Alexander Irving

Short Manual of Heat

For the use of schools and science classes

Alexander Irving

Short Manual of Heat
For the use of schools and science classes

ISBN/EAN: 9783337240981

Printed in Europe, USA, Canada, Australia, Japan

Cover: Foto ©Paul-Georg Meister /pixelio.de

More available books at **www.hansebooks.com**

A SHORT MANUAL
OF
HEAT

FOR the USE of SCHOOLS and SCIENCE CLASSES

BY THE
REV. A. IRVING
B.A. AND B.Sc.

LECTURER ON EXPERIMENTAL AND NATURAL SCIENCE AT WELLINGTON COLLEGE
LATE SECOND MASTER OF THE NOTTINGHAM HIGH SCHOOL

SIXTH EDITION

LONDON
LONGMANS, GREEN, AND CO.
AND NEW YORK : 15 EAST 16th STREET
1888

All rights reserved

PREFACE

TO

THE SECOND EDITION.

THIS little book (as was stated on its first appearance) is an attempt to explain and illustrate briefly the theory of Energy in the various phenomena with which Heat is concerned.

It was thought that by preferring the method here adopted to a more purely deductive method of treating the subject, the wants of a greater number of readers would be met; and the favorable notices which the First Edition received from the Press go to show that this was a reasonable assumption. In revising the work, therefore, for the Second Edition, it has not seemed desirable to make any alterations in its general scope and plan, which is that of an outline of the subject, to be amplified as the teacher may wish. One or two important additions have been made to the last chapter, so as to render its statements more scientifically exact without much increasing its bulk, and here and there throughout the text a few corrections have been made. Answers to the numerical examples have been inserted in the present edition, so as to increase the usefulness of the book for school purposes; and, to gain space for these, some less important terms have been struck out of the Glossary.

The liquefaction of the gases by M. Cailletet and M. Pictet has necessitated the entire re-writing of Article 62, which has been expanded into a short *résumé* of the work done in that important department of Physics. Through the obliging courtesy of M. Cailletet, who has supplied me with information respecting his work, I have been able to do this more satisfactorily than I could otherwise have done; and to that gentleman I beg hereby to express my most grateful acknowledgments.

A. I.

WELLINGTON COLLEGE: *April* 1878.

IN the Third Edition only a few minor alterations have been made.

July 1879.

CONTENTS.

CHAPTER I.

NATURE AND SOURCES OF HEAT.

	PAGE
Mechanical Sources	6
Physical Sources	8
Chemical Sources	10

CHAPTER II.

EXPANSION AND THERMOMETRY.

General Illustration of the Principle of Expansion	14
Thermometers	15
Expansion of Gases	23
,, Solids	29
,, Liquids	35

CHAPTER III.

CHANGES OF PHYSICAL CONDITION.

Liquefaction of Solids	41
Fusion	41
Solution	44
Vaporisation	46
Evaporation	47
Ebullition	58
Chemical Dissociation	63

CHAPTER IV.

CONDUCTION OF HEAT

PAGE 65

CHAPTER V.

SPECIFIC HEAT

74

CHAPTER VI.

RADIANT ENERGY.

Dark and Luminous Heat	83
Radiation	85
Absorption	87
Reflection	89

CHAPTER VII.

HEAT AND WORK.

Conservation and Dissipation of Energy	93

Note I. On the Tension of Water-Vapour	97
Note II. On the Metric System	98
Note III. Davy's 'Kinetic' Theory of Heat	99
Note IV. Bunsen's Calorimeter	100
Note V. Crookes' Radiometer	101
Glossary of Technical Terms	102
Questions and Problems	108
Answers	125
Index	126

HEAT

CHAPTER I.

NATURE AND SOURCES OF HEAT.

1. HEAT is that by which a certain well-known sensation is produced in the human body. Everyone is familiar with the sensations 'hot' and 'cold,' as we express them in ordinary language. Strictly speaking there is no such thing as cold, the term *cold* connoting the comparative absence of heat, as the term *dark* connotes the absence of light. Heat pervades all matter, but in various degrees, and can be transmitted from one body to another. When therefore the surface of the human body is in contact with air or any other substance which is hotter for the time than the body's surface, we experience the sensation of warmth or heat; on the other hand, contact with a colder body causes the sensation of cold; the latter arising from the loss of heat from the human body, as the sensation of warmth follows from an accession of heat to it. But the human body, as well as all other forms of matter, is continually giving off heat; so that the sensation of heat occurs when the adjacent body imparts to the human body more heat than the latter gives off, and the contrary is the case when the sensation of cold is experienced.

2. Before we can obtain a clear notion of the **nature of heat** we must consider the *divisibility of matter*. Let us

take, for example, a lump of common salt (sodium chloride). This may be broken or crushed into very small fragments, and these may be further subdivided by dissolving the salt in water. But there is a limit to this process of subdivision. Thus far each particle held in solution is salt, as may be shown by evaporating the water, so as to leave the salt behind in the form of crystals. Now the smallest possible particle of this salt contains an atom of the metal sodium, combined with an atom of the non-metallic element chlorine: this minutest portion of salt (as such) is called its **molecule**. The molecule may be split up by chemical action, and its elementary **atoms** separated from one another, the chlorine passing off either free or in combination with another element —hydrogen, for example—but the sodium and the chlorine, when separated from each other, have no longer any of the properties of the salt. Also by burning a piece of sodium in a jar of chlorine gas common salt may be produced. In like manner, each molecule of water—whether it be in the solid state (ice), in the liquid state (water), or in the gaseous state (steam or vapour)—is a combination of one atom of oxygen with two atoms of hydrogen They both differ from water in some important respects, the latter being highly combustible, the former the chief supporter of combustion; and if a jet of hydrogen be burnt in oxygen, water is produced by the combination of their atoms.

All those matters which have to do with the relations of the atoms to one another, within the molecule, belong to the science of Chemistry; the investigation of the laws which govern the relations of entire molecules to one another belongs to the domain of Physics. The study of the phenomena and the laws of Heat is a province of the latter science, and forms one of its most important branches.

3. So far as human knowledge goes, the whole universe **is** pervaded by **energy**. This is manifested in various

forms: e.g. the energy of gravitation, by which bodies are drawn towards the earth's centre; the energy of muscular contraction, by virtue of which animals are capable of motion and locomotion; the energy of a body in motion; the energy of chemical affinity, by which the atoms are combined into the molecule.

Heat is a form of energy differing from all these. Besides the motion of a body from one point in space to another, there is a motion within the body of its molecules; but so minute are these that their motion is imperceptible to the sight, even when it is aided by the most powerful microscopes; for, when examined by these, the molecules of a hot body are to all appearance as quiescent as those of a cold one. We may define heat theoretically as a **form of energy consisting of motion in the molecules**; or, more briefly, heat is **molecular motion.** When we say, then, that all bodies in nature possess heat in some degree or other, we mean simply that there is a certain agitation going on, more or less violently, in the molecules of every body. The hotter a body is, the more violently are its molecules agitated.

4. All bodies in nature are Solids or Fluids: either they have a certain definite, more or less rigid, form, which is due to cohesive power holding the molecules together, so as to prevent their separation without the exertion of an appreciable amount of force, in which case the body is a *solid*; or the body has no definite form, and its particles may be separated or moved among one another by exceedingly small forces, in which case the body is a *fluid.* In solids each molecule, though in motion, is confined within a certain very minute space; in fluids there is no such limit to the excursions of the molecule. In solids the molecules grip one another tightly by molecular attraction; in fluids this is overcome by the introduction of the counteracting form of energy, which forms the subject of this little treatise. At present it must be borne in mind that *rigidity*, or resistance

to change of form, is the one characteristic of solids, and the *absence* of this quality that which universally characterises fluids.

Fluids occur either as (1) Liquids or (2) Gases and Vapours. If we partially fill a vessel with water or any other liquid, the air above the liquid is separated from it by a certain distinct surface; and the same is true for liquids generally. If now we exhaust a closed vessel and introduce a small quantity of any gas or vapour, this will not go to the bottom of the vessel, as a liquid would do, but will expand uniformly until it fills the vessel, and exerts equal pressure on all parts of its internal surface; and this is a property common to all *vapours* and *gases*. Bodies of the latter class cannot therefore be kept in an open-mouthed vessel, as a liquid can be, because of their *diffusion*.

All forms of matter, then, must exist in one or other of these conditions, or in those intermediate stages in which a body may exist while passing from one condition to another. As a rule, solids may be converted into liquids, and liquids into gases, by passing heat into them.

The diffusion of gases is explained by considering the gaseous body to consist of a 'great number of molecules moving with very great velocity.'[1]

5. When a cold body is placed in contact with a hotter one, some of the heat of the latter passes into the colder body; in other words, the molecular agitation in the colder body is rendered more violent; and this is often manifest to our senses by a rise of 'temperature' in the colder body. As a result, too, of the increase of heat the whole mass becomes somewhat greater. In the transference of heat from a hot body to a colder one, the effect is really due to the *excess* of heat passing one way over that which is passing the other way; and this depends upon the ratio of the heat of the one to that of the other at the moment of contact. Thus, if one hand be plunged into hot water, and if then

[1] Professor Maxwell, *Theory of Heat*.

both be immersed in water somewhat cooler than the first, but yet warmer than the experimenter's body, the same water will convey the sensation of *warmth* to the one hand and of *cold* to the other at the same time. The heat which a body possesses capable of being transmitted to a colder body is its **temperature**: a body capable of imparting much heat to surrounding objects is said to have a 'high' temperature; one capable of imparting only a small quantity of heat, a 'low' temperature. Three results may follow from subjecting a body to the influence of heat :—

(1) Rise of temperature.
(2) Expansion. (See Art. 17.)
(3) Change of state. (See Ch. III.)

In general the first is accompanied by the second, and often followed by the third.

A rise of temperature in a solid body causes a certain slight expansion; if the same rise of temperature occurs in a liquid, the proportionate increase of volume is greater, while the expansion of gases far exceeds that of liquids. These facts furnish us with a ready means of estimating the temperature of bodies. We are familiar with the fact that glass expands on the application of heat, from the 'click' which accompanies the fracture of glass vessels, when the inner layers of glass are made to expand suddenly from contact with a hot liquid. If a thin glass bulb be filled with a liquid and heated externally, the heat will pass through the glass to the liquid within. The glass will expand only slightly, the liquid much more; and if the bulb be hermetically sealed the internal pressure will cause it to burst. Now if, instead of being sealed, the bulb be joined to a tube so that the bore of the tube be continuous with the interior of the bulb, the excess of the expansion of the liquid over that of the glass envelope will force a portion of the contents into the tube. And if the bore be very small the lengthening of the liquid thread which it contains will be appreciable even for very small increments of heat to the liquid. If, further, the bore of the tube be of the same calibre all the way through, and the tube be marked on the outside with equal spaces or degrees, it is clear that we may compare the temperature imparted to the liquid at one time with that imparted to it at another by noting the number of degrees traversed by the end of the liquid thread in the two instances. Such an instrument is called a *Thermometer* (Gr. θερμός, heat ; μέτρον, measure).

MECHANICAL SOURCES OF HEAT.

6. Everyone is familiar with the fact that by rubbing the hands briskly together a certain amount of heat is generated at the surface of the skin. Why is this? A certain amount of energy is expended in the contraction of the muscles of the arms and hands to set them in motion. This energy of motion, being opposed by the resisting surfaces of the hands, is expended in increasing the agitation of the particles of the skin and of the nerves embedded in it ; and our consciousness of this is the sensation of heat. So when a metal button is rubbed on a deal board, the energy of motion which is given to the button is converted into energy of motion among its particles and those of the wooden surface ; and that this energy is heat is not difficult of demonstration. Again, when a saw is at work—whether the source of its motion be the muscular energy of the mechanic's arm or the expansive force of steam confined within the cylinder of a steam-engine—some of the energy of motion is transformed into molecular energy or heat, by the resisting surfaces of the saw and the wood. This resistance of two surfaces moving in contact is called **friction**.

The amount of heat generated by friction will depend in any case upon three conditions :—

      (1) The force with which the surfaces in contact are pressed together.

      (2) The rapidity of motion of the surfaces in contact.

      (3) The roughness of the surfaces.

By the use of oil—as in machinery, wheels of carriages, &c. —the resistance is made very small and the heat accordingly diminished, the use of the oil being intended to reduce friction as much as possible. The generation of heat by friction has been well illustrated by an experiment of Count Rumford's. Having noticed the heat caused by the boring of cannon, he contrived an apparatus in which a blunt piece of wood was made to rotate while pressed firmly against one end of a copper cylinder. In this way nearly 19 pounds of water contained in the cylinder were made to boil in $2\frac{1}{2}$ hours. One of the most striking instances of heat being produced by friction is that of the partial melting of two lumps of ice when rubbed against each other in a vacuum. Savages are said to procure heat enough to kindle dry grass by rubbing together two pieces of dry wood. Shooting stars, or meteorites, probably owe their brilliancy to the heat engendered by rapid friction against the particles of the atmosphere.

7. If a lump of metal be flattened by a blow from a sledge hammer, the energy of the hammer in motion is, at the moment of the blow, diffused through the mass of the metal and that of the hammer, rendering more violent the agitation of their constituent molecules, as is shown by a rise of temperature. Heat, therefore, is produced by **percussion**. In a waterfall the energy of motion of the 'head of water' is arrested at the bottom and distributed among the molecules of the water; and, as a consequence, the water is somewhat warmer at the bottom than at the top. So the temperature of mercury may be raised by pouring it to and fro for several minutes between two glasses protected from the heat of the hands. Again, on striking a flint and steel, as in the old-fashioned fire-locks, the collision produces so much heat as to render the particles struck off incandescent. Some philosophers have supposed that the Sun's heat arises from the percussion caused by the showering down of meteoric matter upon its surface.

8. If an air-tight piston be forced into a closed cylinder, the **compression** of the air inside generates heat; and in this way sufficient heat may be produced to ignite a piece of German tinder or the vapour of carbon disulphide. Such an apparatus is usually known as the *Pneumatic Syringe.* The compression of air in an ordinary pair of bellows gives it a higher temperature when it issues from the nozzle than when it enters the bellows.

9. Energy in either of the three forms here referred to can be transmitted from one body to another by mechanical contrivances, and may, as we have seen, be expended in producing heat. Friction, pressure, and percussion are therefore *mechanical sources of heat.*

PHYSICAL SOURCES OF HEAT.

10. The chief source of heat to all the planets of our system is the sun. It has been calculated that the heat given off by the sun in an hour is sufficient to liquefy a stratum of ice 2,400 ft. thick, and is equal to what would be produced by burning a layer of solid coal 10 ft. thick enveloping the sun's surface. Of this only $\frac{1}{2300000000}$ is received by the earth; yet the whole amount received in a year is sufficient to melt a layer of ice 35 yds. thick spread over the whole of the earth's surface.[1] What the actual cause of all this heat is has scarcely been satisfactorily determined. **Solar heat** never penetrates the crust of the earth beyond a certain depth, and is given off again into space.

11. The earth contains a large amount of heat within itself, the necessary result of the pressure which results from the force of gravitation; and this is generally spoken of as **terrestrial heat.** As we penetrate below the surface we get farther and farther from the influence of solar heat, until at length this ceases to be felt, and a line of *constant temperature* is reached. The depth of this varies of course in

---

[1] Professor Tyndall, *Heat as a Mode of Motion.*

different latitudes : at Paris it is about 90 ft. On penetrating below this line it is found that the terrestrial heat increases with the depth at the rate of about 1 deg. Cent. for every 90 ft.; from which we infer that at the depth of 20 or 30 miles the heat must be very great indeed. This inference is confirmed (1) by the action of volcanoes, which, during eruptions, discharge steam, molten rocks, and red-hot 'ash' from a great depth; (2) by the temperature of hot springs and geysers; (3) by the temperature of the water which issues from artesian wells.

12. One form in which energy is exhibited is electricity. Through some substances (as, e.g., copper wire) this kind of energy passes with little resistance, while other substances ('bad conductors') offer considerable resistance to the pas-

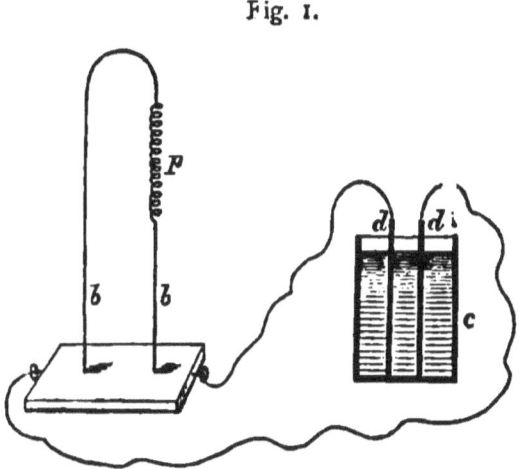

Fig. 1.

sage of electricity. Being thus opposed in its course, electricity is converted into heat, and this is sometimes so great as, in the case of lightning, to set buildings on fire. **Electrical resistance** is therefore a source of heat.

This will be better understood by reference to the accompanying diagram (Fig. 1). At c is indicated a cell of a battery. The acid contained in the cell acts upon the metallic plates $d\,d$, and when the plates are connected by a wire, a current of electricity passes through the acidulated water, the plates, and the wire. If the wires connected with the plates be also connected with any apparatus, which is a good couductor of electricity, the current will still continue, the circuit being unbroken. Suppose them connected with the two upright copper wires *b b*, and that these are connected at *p* by a coil of wire of the metal *platinum*, which is a poor conductor of electricity. The current is interfered with by the greater *resistance* which the platinum offers to it, and the result is that the coil is soon seen to glow with a white heat. It is easy to see how such a device may be applied for igniting gas and firing mines or torpedoes by electricity.

CHEMICAL SOURCES OF HEAT.

13. The source of heat with which we are most familiar is a common fire. Let us consider what we mean when we say, 'The fire is burning.' The fuel, whether wood, or coal, or peat, contains a quantity of combustible matter. By this we must not understand that it is capable of destruction, for *matter is indestructible*. The combustible parts of the fuel are bodies which, by combination with the oxygen of the atmosphere, form invisible gases together with water-vapour. These are generally diffused through the air as fast as they are formed; but by a proper arrangement a given weight of fuel may be completely burnt, and all the products of combustion collected and weighed. When the weight of these aëriform products of combustion is added to that of the ash (which is so much incombustible earthy matter, and consequently not fuel, but an impurity present in the fuel) it is found not only that there is no loss, but a considerable *increase* of weight above that of the fuel consumed. This extra weight is due to the oxygen which, in the process of *combustion*, has combined with the constituents of the fuel (mainly carbon and hydrogen). But in combining the atoms of these various elements rush together with a force

greater than anything we can conceive, and the clashing of them at the moment of contact gives rise to that form of molecular energy which we call heat. A similar process goes on in a candle or gas flame. In both these cases it is a gas that is burning, the difference between the wick of a candle and a gas-jet being that the former is its own gas-producer. The gas in each case is composed mainly of carbon and hydrogen, the former of which occurs free in nature only in the solid state, as diamond, graphite, &c.; the latter being the lightest of all known substances. Oxygen, having great attraction for both these elementary bodies, combines vigorously with them, and this **chemical combination** is the source of the heat of the flame.

In Fig. 2 the three regions generally observable in a

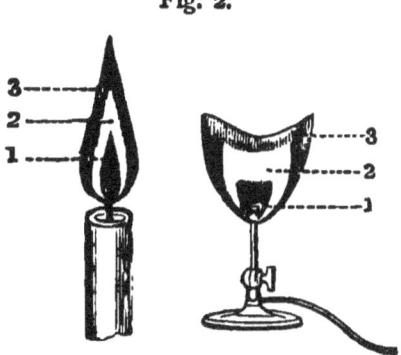

Fig. 2.

candle or gas-flame are represented. The dark region (1) is occupied by the gas in a highly heated state, but as yet *unburnt*. Now, the particles of a gas being, as we have seen, always in rapid motion, some of the oxygen of the air in the vicinity of the flame must penetrate into the flame and come into contact with this hot gas. Here it combines, in the first instance, with the hydrogen, producing intensely hot steam, and the particles of carbon, being liberated and floating freely in this heated gas, are in region (2) raised to a white heat and give out *light*. As these hot carbon atoms pass outwards they, in their turn, combine with the oxygen which floats about the flame, and a gas known as carbonic anhydride (carbon dioxide) is formed in region (3). By the oxidation, first of the hydrogen, and then of the carbon, the heat of the flame is produced.

14. When a strong current of air comes in contact with a gas flame, the oxygen is carried forcibly to the interior of the flame, and thus the region of entire combustion is extended inwards, so as to wholly or partially obliterate the region of partial combustion. We consequently get less light but more heat from the flame, as is well known to those who are familiar with the use of the blow-pipe. In the Bunsen burner the same principle is turned to account, an arrangement being made for allowing the air to enter the tube, and mingle with the coal gas, before the latter issues from the burner. The oxyhydrogen flame gives even greater heat.

15. In ordinary language light, as well as heat, is regarded as an accompaniment of combustion. In a scientific sense, however, the word 'combustion' does not necessarily imply this, and we must accordingly extend our notion of *burning* so as to include some instances in which that variety of energy which is capable of exciting the sensation of light in the retina of the eye is not produced. The most important and interesting instance is that which occurs within the animal body.

The temperature of warm-blooded animals (of man, for example) has to be constantly maintained considerably above that of the surrounding air, and to this end a process of *slow combustion* goes on within. The food eaten and the waste matter of the tissues furnish the fuel. The blood, having absorbed oxygen in its passage through the lungs, carries this on through the body. In this way oxygen is supplied to the carbonaceous matter, and the oxidation of the carbon furnishes animal heat. When we climb a hill, we produce more heat than when we walk the same distance along a level road; for in the former case more muscle is expended in lifting the body, and by increased rapidity of respiration oxygen is conveyed more rapidly through the body, the result of which is an acceleration of the internal process of combustion: hence the greater heat. The same gas (carbonic anhydride) is produced by slow combustion within the body as is produced in an ordinary flame, which may easily be shown. For by means of an 'aspirator' the current of air from a candle or gas flame may be made to pass through a tube containing a perfectly clear solution of lime. The carbonic anhydride combines with the lime to form a carbonate (chalk). This is insoluble in the water, which is therefore rendered turbid. Exactly the same effect is produced when breath from the lungs is blown through a perfectly clear solution of lime.

16. Not only is oxidation a source of heat, as in the different cases we have just considered, but heat is the invariable result of all cases of chemical combination. A familiar instance of this is seen in the heat which is generated, when, in making mortar, the bricklayer's labourer pours water upon quick lime; the heat results from the combination of the water with the lime. Again, if cold oil of vitriol be poured into cold water contained in a glass beaker, the heat caused by the combination of these two cold liquids is so great as often to make the glass too hot to be held in the hand. In cases of what is usually known as 'spontaneous combustion,' heat is produced by chemical action; and there is little doubt that many destructive fires originate in this way, especially from the storage of damp carbonaceous materials.

To the above cases of chemical action (Arts. 13–16) may be added that which takes place at two stages in the life-history of an ordinary plant: (1) When germination goes on in the seed; (2) when the flower-bud is opening: in both cases heat is produced, oxygen is used up, and carbon dioxide is given off. The first fact is one which is known to every maltster.

CHAPTER II.

EXPANSION AND THERMOMETRY.

17. SPEAKING generally, whenever heat passes from a hot body into a colder one, the body which receives an accession of heat is found to occupy a larger volume than before; this is what is meant by the 'expansion of heat.'

Thus if a ball of metal be made of such a size as to exactly fit a ring of the same material, when the two are at the ordinary temperature of the air, it will be found, on heating the ball, that it no longer passes through the ring, unless the latter be

Fig. 3.

heated to the same temperature as the ball. In Fig. 3 the heated ball is shown supported by the ring, the ball being hotter than the ring; but as soon as the temperature of the ball cools down to that of the ring, the ball falls through. This piece of simple apparatus is known as *Gravesande's Ring*.

Next let us take a tube of glass, with a good-sized bulb blown at one end, and let us fill the bulb and part of the tube with some liquid, coloured so as to make the termination of the liquid thread more distinctly visible. When the tube, with its contents, is plunged into hot water, two things are observed. (1) The immediate result is a slight lowering of the liquid in the tube, because the heat from the surrounding water, acting first upon the glass envelope, expands this before it has time to penetrate into the liquid; and as the bulb expands some of the liquid in the tube descends to fill up the additional space inside. (2) The descent of the liquid is slight; it remains for a moment stationary, and afterwards rises to a point higher than that at which it stood at first. Heat passing into the liquid expands it.

Expansion of gases may be illustrated by a still simpler experiment. Suppose the tube filled with air instead of a liquid, and let this air be separated from the external air by a small portion of liquid in the bore of the tube; the mere application of the hands will furnish heat enough to drive this drop of liquid through the tube, by the expansion of the internal air. Or we may vary the experiment by having the tube quite clear and putting the open end of it under water before applying the hands to the bulb; in this case the expansion of the air inside will force some of it out into the water, and it will rise in bubbles to the surface. [See Art. 24.]

THERMOMETERS.[1]

18. *To Fill a Thermometer.*—The bore of the tube should be as nearly as possible of uniform calibre throughout. In most thermometers the bore is so small that the liquid (generally mercury) to be passed into it will not enter, because the space does not admit of the passage of the liquid one way and the internal air the other, and because there is a certain amount of repulsion between glass and mercury, giving a convex form to the end of a column of the latter when it is contained in a glass tube. We must make use, therefore, of the law of expansion. (1) The open

[1] See Art. 5.

end of the tube represented in Fig. 4 is plunged beneath the surface of mercury contained in an open vessel, while, by means of a spirit lamp, the bulb b' is heated, so as to expel some of the air which it contains; and this escapes in bubbles through the liquid. When this bulb is allowed to cool by removing the lamp, the pressure of the external air drives a quantity of the liquid mercury into the bulb b. In this way this bulb may be nearly filled. (2) The tube is placed erect, as in the figure, and the bulb b' again heated.

Fig. 4.

The expelled air rises this time in bubbles through the liquid in b; and when b' is again cooled, the liquid in b descends into b'. This is repeated until b' and a portion of the tube are filled with mercury; and by heating the bulb b' to boiling, all the air in the tube is expelled by the vapour of mercury. The bulb b is then removed and the tube hermetically sealed by the blow-pipe flame, without allowing any air to enter.

19. *To Graduate a Thermometer.*—For this purpose two *fixed points* are wanted; the first is the ordinary temperature

Construction of Thermometers.

of pure freezing water, the second the ordinary temperature of pure boiling water, both taken at the average pressure which the atmosphere exerts at the mean sea level. (Art. 32.)

The **freezing-point** is first ascertained, by immersing the upright closed tube in a vessel of moist snow or pounded ice; the mercury sinks, and at last becomes stationary, and the point thus indicated is scratched on the glass tube.

To obtain the **boiling-point** the tube is placed in a vessel full of steam over boiling water, and protected by a 'steam-jacket' from the cooling effects of the external air; the point to which the liquid thread of mercury rises is marked on the tube.

The distance between these two fixed points is the *unit of thermometry*. It is clear that this space may be divided into different numbers of equal parts or '*degrees;*' and this gives rise to different *scales of graduation*.

In the **Centigrade scale** the space between the fixed points is divided into 100 parts, and the F.P. is marked 0°.

In the **Fahrenheit scale** the space between the fixed points is divided into 180 parts, and F.P. is marked 32°.

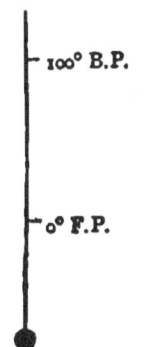
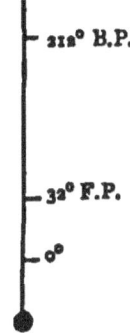

Hence we have the following formulæ [1] for **conversion** of 'readings' from one scale to the other :—

---

[1] The application of these formulæ requires some slight acquaintance with the first rules of algebra, since temperatures below 0° in each scale are expressed as *negative quantities*.

$32 \pm \frac{9}{5}$(No. of degs. Cent.)=No. of degs. Fahr.

$\frac{5}{9}$(No. of degs. Fahr.-32)=No. of degs. Cent.

The zero in the Fahr. scale corresponds to the temperature of a mixture of ice and salt. (Comp. Art. 53.)

There are also thermometers in which Réaumur's graduation is adopted, the fixed space being divided into 80 degrees. The Centigrade scale (introduced by Celsius) is adopted in most scientific treatises and investigations in this country, and on the Continent.

For very low temperatures (below about $-36°$ Cent.) mercury becomes useless, on account of its congelation at $-39°$. Alcohol, which has never been known to freeze at any temperature, is then usually substituted for the metal.

20. *Displacement of the Freezing-point.*

(1) When a thermometer has been suddenly transferred from a hot to a cold temperature, the F.P. often stands a fraction of a degree lower, as owing to the sudden cooling of the glass bulb it has not contracted to exactly its former size. This is why the F.P. must be fixed before the B.P.

(2) In course of time the F.P. may rise from a compression of the bulb due to the pressure of the air upon a body of the nature of glass, which is to some degree plastic. Very delicate instruments are therefore often filled two or three years before being graduated.

The errors arising from the displacement of the F.P. (2) are greatly magnified, when to the pressure of the atmosphere is added that of a column of water many hundred fathoms deep, as occurs in ascertaining the temperature of the sea at great depths. To obviate this the tube is enclosed within a second one; the space between them is *partly* filled with alcohol, which facilitates the equalisation of the temperature of the internal mercury and the external water. The rest of the intervening space contains air, which is easily compressed. Under these circumstances the pressure upon the external tube is not communicated to the internal one.

Other sources of error :—

(1) Not exposing the bulb and stem, when used, to the same degree of temperature.

(2) Not using the instrument in the same position in which it was graduated.

(3) Unequal expansion of different kinds of glass.

(4) Slight variations of different parts of the bore of the tube. As this occurs even in the best tubes, they must, when great nicety is required, be *calibrated*. This is done by passing a short thread of mercury along the tube, and marking the variations of its length. But the most reliable means of rendering the readings of different thermometers strictly comparable, is to correct each one by a standard thermometer, such as that at the Kew Observatory.

Fig. 5.

21. **Differential Thermometer.**—This instrument is used to ascertain the *difference* between the temperatures of two bodies or places near each other.

Fig. 5 represents Leslie's differential thermometer, which consists of a glass tube bent twice at right angles, each arm ending in a hollow glass bulb, *a, b*.

The liquid, which is dilute sulphuric acid tinged red with litmus, is poured in at *c*, and the tube is then hermetically sealed. When the air in the bulbs has been equalised, the liquid will stand at the same level in both arms; this is indicated by 0°. If, then, one bulb be heated more than the other, the expansion of the air will force the liquid down in that arm, and it will rise a corresponding height in the other. Let *a* be heated, say, 10° more than *b*, and the point at which the liquid stands marked; then reverse the process by heating *b* 10° more than *a*, and marking in a similar way. The space above and below 0° is divided into 10 parts or degrees, generally marked on the frame.

Rumford's has a small drop of liquid in the horizontal tube, to which the degrees are attached.

22. Maximum and Minimum Thermometers are so constructed as to be *self-registering*; the former being used to show the greatest heat during the day, the latter the greatest cold during the night. They are usually constructed so as to be used horizontally, and the simplest form of them is shown in Fig. 6.

The upper represents a maximum thermometer, and con-

Fig. 6.

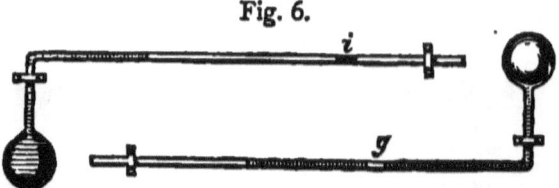

tains *mercury*; the lower a minimum thermometer, and contains *alcohol*. When the mercury expands, it pushes a little iron bead *i* along, and *leaves it there on contracting again*. When the alcohol contracts, it draws the glass bead *g* with it by adhesion; but on expanding again passes between it and the tube, and so the lowest temperature is registered by the position of *g*. The readings are obtained from graduated scales, which are generally upon the tablet to which the tubes are affixed for suspension.

23. Breguet's Metallic Thermometer.—In this the unequal expansion of platinum (the least expansible metal) and silver (one of the most expansible) is turned to account.

A triple ribbon is made by soldering together a strip of silver, a strip of gold, and a strip of platinum, the gold being between the other two. This is then made into a spiral coil, which is suspended at one end; the other end having an index attached, which moves horizontally over a circular dial, on which the degrees are marked by trial with an ordinary thermometer. The coil is so made that the silver is on the interior, and the platinum on the exterior. When the temperature of the coil rises, the silver expands faster than the platinum, and deflects the needle in one direction; when it falls, the more speedy contraction of the silver deflects the needle in the opposite direction.

24. **Air Thermometer.**—This, the oldest form of thermometer (the invention of which is ascribed to Galileo), is still used for some purposes. It consists of a glass tube, of which one end is expanded into a bulb, the open end dipping beneath the surface of a liquid. When the closed end is heated, the expanding air drives the liquid through the tube, to a distance which varies according to the temperature. This is a useful form of pyrometer, for ascertaining the heat of a furnace, platinum or porcelain being substituted for glass. The advantages of the air thermometer are that it indicates very small increments and decrements of temperature, and that gaseous bodies expand uniformly (which liquids do not) through a very great range of temperature. As, however, its action is modified by the pressure of the external atmosphere, its indications must be corrected by reference to the barometer: it is therefore much less convenient for most purposes than the mercurial thermometer, though of great use in many important scientific experiments.

25. **The Thermo-pile.**—It is a fact that, if two pieces of different metals be soldered together, and the junction heated, a current of electricity passes from one to the other, the direction of the current being reversed during cooling.

In the following 'thermo-electric series' of metals a positive current will pass when any one of the metals in the list is joined to any that follow.[1] These are:

[1] Prof. Balfour Stewart, *Treatise on Heat*

Bismuth	Copper	Iron
Nickel	Platinum	Antimony
Lead	Silver	Tellurium
Tin	Zinc	

In the construction of the thermo-pile, bismuth, the first, is generally used along with antimony, the last but one of the list. About 25 couples of these two metals are formed into a square block or 'pile,' the junctions of the metals being on the face of the block. Some of these are represented in the

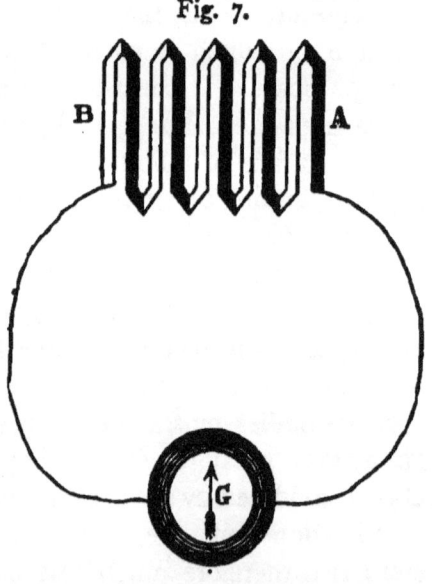

Fig. 7.

series B A (Fig. 7), the dark bars being composed of antimony, the light ones of bismuth. The series is connected by wires with a freely suspended plate G, bearing a magnet, and surrounded with a wire coil. This is called the *galvanometer*. The slightest rise of temperature at the junctions of the metallic bars will cause a current to pass, and this, as it passes round the coil of the galvanometer, deflects the magnet in one direction; on the other hand, a fall of temperature at the junctions of the couples makes a current pass in the opposite direction through the coil, and the deflection of the magnet is reversed. By means of this instrument the slightest variations of temperature in any object presented to the face of the pile are indicated. We cannot here describe all the accessory appliances necessary for the application of this delicate piece of apparatus.

EXPANSION OF GASES.

26. Let us take a metallic cylinder, such as is represented in section at c, Fig. 8, fitted with an air-tight piston

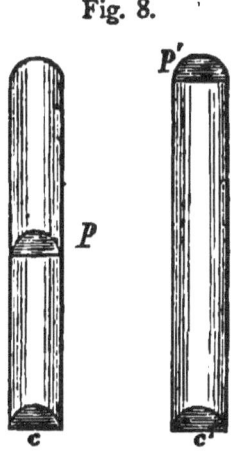

Fig. 8.

p; and let the space below the piston be, say, one cubic foot, their material being supposed to be perfectly impermeable to heat ('adiabatic'). This space we will suppose to be filled with air or some other gas or mixture of gases, so that the expansive force of the air below the piston shall support the pressure of the air above + the weight of the piston. This expansive force is due to the energy with which the molecules encounter the internal surface of the vessel. Now if the piston be raised, so that the space contained below it becomes doubled (2 cub. ft. instead of 1), as at c', and if the piston be held in the position p', what is the result? The number of molecules inside the enclosed space is the same as before, when the space allowed for their motion was only half as great; and—the temperature remaining constant—the rapidity of their motion continues unaltered. It follows from these conditions that the number of the molecules that impinge upon an unit of surface in an unit of time is less by one-half in the latter than in the former case: we have doubled the area subject to their bombardment without increasing the force of our artillery. On the other hand, if the piston c be forced down, the resistance of the gas inside increases with the descent of the piston.

The law may be thus stated:

The Volume of a given quantity of gas bears an **inverse** *ratio to the* **pressure** *upon it;*

Or, *The volume of the gas varies as the* **density.**

It is known as the 'law of Boyle,' from its discoverer, a philosopher of the seventeenth century. It was also discovered independently by his contemporary Mariotte, after whom it is named on the Continent.

27. If heat be applied to the cylinder c' the temperature of the gas inside will be raised, the molecules moving now with increased velocity. And if sufficient heat be imparted, the velocity of the molecular motion of the gas may be doubled. As the result of this, the number of molecules which impinge upon an unit of surface in an unit of time will be the same as in the first instance, when at c the gas at a lower temperature filled just half the space. The internal pressure at c' becomes, therefore, the same as at c. This exemplifies the following 'law of Charles':—

The Volume of a given quantity of gas bears a **direct** *ratio to its* **temperature.**

Air and gases generally increase by $\frac{1}{273}$ of their volume at 0° C. for each degree of rise of temperature.

This is called the **coefficient of expansion, or factor of expansion.** It follows (theoretically) that if a given mass of air were cooled down without being liquefied to the temperature $-273°$ C. it would be reduced to a mathematical point.

This is called, therefore, **absolute zero**, and temperatures reckoned from it **absolute temperatures**. (Comp. Art. 62.)

28. The expansion of gases under the influence of heat is capable of many simple and familiar illustrations.

(*a*) If a *bladder*, partly filled with air and tightly closed, be heated before the fire, the air inside will expand and stretch the bladder to its full dimensions.

(*b*) *Fire balloons* ascend by reason of the expansion of the heated air contained within them.

(*c*) If a flask is made air-tight, then connected by a tube with a jar filled with water and inverted over the *pneumatic trough*, the air, by its expansion, is partly driven over, so as to displace the water in the inverted jar when heat is applied to the flask. In this way gases are often collected, when they are generated by chemical action within the flask, with or without application of heat to the exterior.

(*d*) *Heron's Fountain* is a sort of philosophical toy, which is made to produce a jet of water from a small orifice at the end of a glass tube. The tube is carried down inside a well-corked flask nearly to the bottom, the flask being about half-filled with water. On applying heat to the flask, the expansive energy of the air and of the steam inside drives the water through the tube with considerable force.

29. Application of the law of expansion:

(*a*) The heat of a common fire expands the air above it, and so makes the column of air inside lighter than an equal column of air outside the chimney.

(*b*) The expansive energy of *steam*, which is the motive power in the steam engine, is caused by heat.

(*c*) The explosive force of *gunpowder* is due to the sudden formation of a large quantity of gases in a highly heated state.

(*d*) It is this law that makes the ventilation of rooms, factories, &c., possible. To secure proper **ventilation** arrangements should be made for the warm air of the room to escape near the ceiling, the fresh air being admitted from below. This may be easily shown by holding a lighted taper in the open doorway of a room, the external air being colder than that of the room. When it is held at the top of the doorway the flame is borne outwards; when at the bottom, the flame is borne inwards. Mines are ventilated by furnaces at the bottom of 'up-cast' shafts, which cause a circulation of air through the workings.

(*e*) Large buildings are frequently warmed by means of *hot-air apparatus*. The air which passes over the furnace below the building is expanded by heat and rises through the building. Such an arrangement is often made to serve the double purpose of warming and ventilation.

(*f*) The *air thermometer*. (See Art. 24.)

In the case of a common chimney, it must be borne in mind that the force of the upward current of air mainly depends upon the difference between the temperature of the air inside and of that outside the chimney; the greater this difference the stronger the 'draught.' This explains why (1) a chimney 'draws' better in frosty than in warm weather; (2) a 'blower,' by causing all the air as it enters the chimney to pass through the fire, increases the draught; (3) the chimney draws better after the fire has been burning for some time than when it is first lighted. By increasing the height, the difference of external pressure at top and bottom is increased, and a circular flue is better than a square one, since counter-currents are avoided, and friction is reduced to a minimum.

30. The expansion of gases when heated is the cause of many natural phenomena:—

(1) The *Trade Winds* are a rush of air from N. and S. towards the Equator, where the air is rarefied by heat, and therefore rises. The rush from N. and S. is turned relatively westward by the earth's rotation.

(2) *Land and sea breezes.* When during the day in tropical regions the land is heated more than the adjoining ocean, the air above the land rises, and the sea-breezes rush

landward; on the contrary at night, the land becoming cooler than the water, there is a rush of air seaward.

(3) *Prevailing westerly winds.* The heated air of the tropics rises, and spreading north and south, retains somewhat of the velocity of motion eastward which it acquired in Equatorial regions, until it reaches the surface of the earth in the temperate zones. These winds are known as the *Antitrades.*

(4) *Geysers.* These are intermittent springs or huge jets of boiling water, and their action is the result of the expansive force of steam, formed within the natural tube through which the water escapes.

31. As gases expand when subjected to the influence of heat, so when they are allowed to expand by their own elasticity (i.e. by simply removing the surrounding pressure) a *fall of temperature* is the result. Thus when a body of air largely charged with water-vapour ascends the side of a mountain range, it is relieved more and more from pressure the higher it goes, and its temperature falls accordingly on account of its expansion. This is the reason of the rainfall being more copious in mountain districts than in the plains. The condensation of invisible vapour into a visible cloud by the expansion of air may be shown by partially exhausting a large glass globe by the air-pump.

32. **Density of Gases and Vapours.**—The factor of expansion for aëriform fluids being much greater than those for liquids and solids, it is clear that only a moderate change of their temperature will (at constant pressure) affect very considerably their densities. The '**vapour density**' is always considered with reference to the density of **air** as the standard, and is expressed as some proper or improper fraction of the density of air. For accurate comparison the air and the gas in question must be at the same temperature. But besides this some fixed temperature of air must be accepted as that by which all other temperatures may be corrected; and the temperature selected is that of freezing water, or $0°$ C.

Corrections must also be made for variations of pressure, the mean pressure at the level of the sea being just sufficient to support a column of mercury in the barometer tube 760 mm high. We have, therefore—

Normal temperature, 0° C.
Normal pressure, 760 mm.

The arithmetical factor which expresses the ratio of the density of the gas to the density of air furnishes the **specific gravity** of the gas; if we wish to obtain the **absolute density** of the gas—that is, its density as compared with all other forms of matter whose density can be ascertained—we must multiply the specific gravity (sp. gr.) by that factor which expresses the weight of dry air at normal pressure and temperature measured in the terms of the weight of an equal volume of water when at its maximum density. The unit of weight (gramme) being that of 1 *cub. cm of distilled water at* $4°C.$, and the weight of a *litre* of dry air at normal pressure and temperature being 1·2932 grammes, it is manifest that (1 litre = 1000 ccm) the weight of air as compared with that of water at 4° C. is expressed by the fraction ·0012932.

∴ sp. gr. of gas × ·0012932 = absolute density of gas.

33. Corrections of Volume for Normal Pressure and Temperature.—Let v represent the measured volume of a gas at any *temperature*, and let this temperature be $x°$ above or below the normal temperature.

In the first case, suppose the temperature $x°$ *above* 0° C.; then every 273 ccm of the gas at 0° C. will, at the given temperature, occupy $(273+x)$ ccm. When, therefore, the temperature of the gas is *lowered* to 0° C., its volume will be *diminished* in the ratio of $(273+x) : 273$. (Art. 27.)

In the second case let the temperature of the measured gas be $x°$ *below* 0° C.; then every 273 ccm of the gas at 0° C. will occupy only $(273-x)$ at the given temperature. When, therefore, the gas has its temperature *raised* to 0°C., its volume will be *increased* in the ratio of $(273-x) : 273$.

If, then, we call the corrected volume v, we have (by Art. 27)

$$\mathrm{v} = v \times \frac{273}{273 \pm x} \quad \ldots \quad \ldots \quad (1).$$

To correct for *pressure*, let us suppose the volume of the gas to have been measured at a pressure of the atmosphere which is shown by the barometer to be p mm.

In the first case, let the pressure be *greater* than 760 mm; then on *reducing* this pressure to the normal pressure the gas would *expand* in the ratio of $760 : p$.

In the second case, the pressure being *less* than 760 mm, the gas will, on the pressure being *increased* to 760 mm have its volume *diminished* in the ratio of $760 : p$.

v and v as before, we get

$$\mathrm{v} = v \times \frac{p}{760} \quad \ldots \quad \ldots \quad (2).$$

This formula expresses *Boyle & Mariotte's Law* (Art. 26). Combining (1) and (2),

$$\mathrm{v} = v \times \frac{p}{760} \times \frac{273}{273 \pm x}$$

Note.—To calculate the volume of a gas (measured at 760 mm. and 0° C.) for any other pressure or temperature, invert these fractions.

EXPANSION OF SOLIDS.

34. The expansion of solid bodies has been already illustrated (Art. 17).

Fig. 9.

The expansion of a bar in the direction of its length

('linear' expansion) may be illustrated by Ferguson's *Pyrometer* (Fig. 9.), so called because a bar of metal is sometimes used in this way to estimate the temperature of furnaces, and high temperatures generally, above 350° C., at which mercury boils.

The bar is held securely at a, but allowed to move freely through b; when heated by lamps, or a trough of burning alcohol, placed beneath it, the bar expands and moves the index or pointer c.

Most solids expand pretty evenly for temperatures between those of freezing and boiling water; but all solid substances do not expand equally for equal increments of temperature. A rod of glass which measures 1 ft. at 0° C., will measure 1·000008 ft. at 1° C. If we take the difference (·000008 ft.) of these dimensions, this decimal will represent the expansion in the direction of the bar's length caused by a rise of temperature of 1° C. This quantity ·000008 therefore is the *coefficient of expansion of glass*. Similarly a bar of zinc 1 ft. long at 0° C. will measure at 1° C. 1·000029 ft.; so that the coefficient of expansion of zinc is ·000029. The coefficients of expansion of the ordinary metals lie between these limits. (Art. 38.)

35. The simplest method of obtaining the coefft. of linear expansion is that of Lavoisier & Laplace.

Fig. 10.

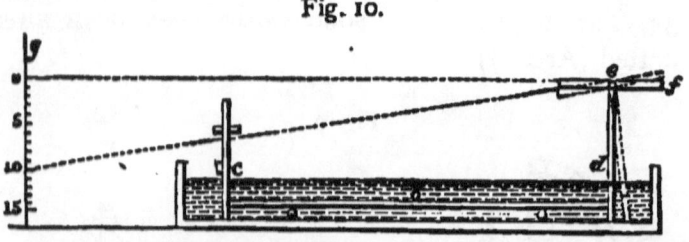

In Fig. 10 let a represent the section of a trough containing water or oil in which the bar b is placed on small rollers, meeting a firmly fixed upright plate c at one end, while the other end is in contact with a bar d attached at right angles to a horizontal bar, which is seen in section at e, and at the end of this is fastened a small telescope f. At g is a vertical line graduated. When the telescope is horizontal, the experimenter, applying his eye to it, reads zero on the graduated scale. Let heat be now applied to the vessel from beneath; as the liquid gets hotter the bar of metal does so too, and by means of a thermometer we can ascertain how many degrees the liquid has risen in temperature, which will of course show also the increase of temperature of the bar. But at the same time this will have increased in length and have pushed the bar d to the right through a certain angle. The telescope must revolve through the same angle, and the experimenter will now read the No. of degrees on the scale. The distance from e to the scale is known, also the vertical distance from e to the bar; hence from similar triangles the following proportion—Distance from e to scale : distance read off on scale :: distance d : whole expansion of b.

$$\frac{\text{Whole expansion of } b}{\text{No. of degs. rise of temperature}} = \text{coefft. of expansion}$$

For most solids the coefficient of expansion is found to increase considerably when they are heated much above 100° C.

36. The 'superficial expansion' of a plane surface will be got from the following expression:—

$$\left(1+\frac{1}{x}\right)^2 = 1 + \frac{2}{x} + \frac{1}{x^2}$$

in which $\frac{1}{x}$ represents the linear expansion, expressed as a fraction of the length at a temperature 1° lower. The value of this fraction is, as we have seen (Art. 34), very small for the metals and most other solids; and therefore the value of $\frac{1}{x^2}$ is so exceedingly small that it may be left out of account altogether, and the superficial expansion is shown, to a sufficient degree of accuracy, by $\frac{2}{x}$. We get, therefore, the following rule for obtaining the superficial expansion of a solid substance when its linear expansion is known :—

Superficial expansion = 2 × *linear expansion*.

37. Again, if $1 + \frac{1}{x}$ represent as before the length of a solid body which has been subjected to heat, its length at a temperature 1° lower being represented by unity, we have the cubical dimension of the heated body shown by the expression—

$$\left(1 + \frac{1}{x}\right)^3 = 1 + \frac{3}{x} + \frac{3}{x^2} + \frac{1}{x^3}.$$

Here the value of $\frac{3}{x^2} + \frac{1}{x^3}$ is exceedingly small, and may be neglected, so that $\frac{3}{x}$ may be considered a sufficiently accurate expression for the 'cubical expansion' of the body. We therefore get the following expression for obtaining the cubical expansion when the linear expansion is known :—

Cubical expansion = 3 × *linear expansion*.

38. *Coefficients of Linear Expansion for* 1°, *between* 0° *and* 100° C.

White glass	·0000086
Platinum	·0000088
Steel (untempered)	·0000108
Cast iron	·0000112
Wrought iron	·0000122
Steel (tempered)	·0000124
Gold	·0000147
Copper	·0000172
Bronze	·0000182
Brass	·0000188
Silver	·0000191
Tin	·0000217
Lead	·0000286
Zinc	·0000294

Practical Application.

39. As a solid body increases its bulk when heated, so (if time be allowed) it regains its original volume on cooling. If cooled too quickly its particles do not resume their proper position with regard to one another, and the substance is rendered on that account more brittle. Hence the necessity of *annealing* in glass-working. *Rupert's Drops* illustrate this. They are small lumps of glass which have been suddenly solidified by dropping molten glass into a cold liquid. If one of these be scratched, or its point broken, the whole lump flies into a fine powder.

Some *crystallised* substances expand more in one direction than another when heated, according to the position of the crystalline axes.

40. The expansion of solids under the influence of heat is a most important consideration in engineering and the arts :—

(1) Iron bars of furnaces must be free at one end.

(2) Allowance must be made in iron girders of bridges for expansion in summer.

(3) On railways small spaces must be left between the ends of the rails.

(4) Waterpipes must be fitted by telescopic joints.

(5) Glass must not be heated too quickly in one place if we wish to avoid fracture.

(6) *Compensating pendulums* of clocks and the *compensation balances* of chronometers are ingenious contrivances for counteracting the effects of expansion from heat.

The commonest form of compensating pendulum consists of an ordinary pendulum fitted with a cylinder above the bob. This cylinder is partly filled with mercury. When the heat of summer or of a warm room expands the rod of the pendulum, and so *lowers* the bob, the mercury expands *upwards* from the same cause. In this way the distance between the *centre of oscillation* of the whole pendulum and the point at which it is suspended is kept uniform, a condition necessary for the indication of correct time by the clock.

Another form is that of the *Gridiron Pendulum*. The principle of its construction will be readily understood by reference to Fig. 11.

It consists of four upright oblong frames composed alternately of brass and steel. It is clear that if the whole expansion upwards of the brass rods $bbbb$ is just as great as the downward extension of the steel rods $sssss$, the position

Fig. 11.

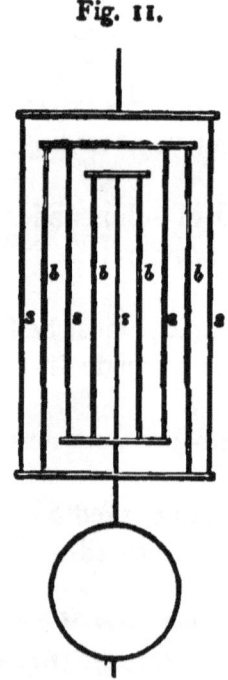

of the bob remains unaltered by changes of temperature. This will be the case when

$$\frac{\text{length of brass rods}}{\text{length of steel rods}} = \frac{\text{coefficient of expansion of steel}}{\text{coefficient of expansion of brass}}.$$

or, length of brass : length of steel :: 124 : 188. (Art. 38.)

41. *Contraction* on cooling has also been applied to useful purposes:—

(1) In securing the tires of wheels. The tire being

put on hot, contracts on cooling, and not only grips the wheel tightly, but drives the spokes more firmly into the felloes and axle-tree, and renders the whole more firm and compact. For the same reason, plates of steam-boilers and of wrought-iron girders are fastened together by red-hot rivets.

(2) Walls of buildings, which have sunk outwards from the perpendicular have been pulled upright by the cooling of iron bars, these having been screwed up tightly on the outside after being heated.

EXPANSION OF LIQUIDS.

42. This property has been illustrated in a general way

Fig. 12.

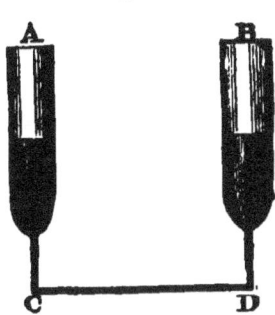

already (Art. 17). It was then noticed that when the tube containing cold water was plunged into hot water, the interior liquid fell slightly at first. This shows that the *apparent* expansion of a liquid, when it is heated in an envelope of glass or other solid material, is not quite so great as its *absolute* expansion. It is therefore important for experiments of great nicety to obtain the absolute expansion of some liquid; so that, by the difference between this and its apparent expansion, the expansion of the interior of the glass may be known with great accuracy. For this purpose mercury is selected; and the following ingenious method was devised by Dulong and Petit for ascertaining the **absolute expansion of mercury.**

Two tubes were taken (A and B, Fig. 12) of equal dimensions and connected by a tube C D having a very small bore. When the temperature of the tubes is equal, the mercury must stand at the same level in both, according to the general law for the equilibrium of fluids in communicating vessels. Suppose the horizontal tube bisected by a vertical plane; then the pressures on both sides of this plane must exactly counterbalance each other, so long as equilibrium is maintained. From this it follows that if one of the tubes, as B D, be heated more than the other A C, equilibrium can only be maintained by the column of mercury standing at a higher level in B D than in A C, in the *inverse ratio of their densities*. In the experiment of Dulong the tube A C was surrounded by a freezing mixture; the other tube B D by a cylinder of oil, so arranged as to be heated by a small furnace, the temperature to which the oil (and consequently the mercury in B D) was raised in each instance being known by thermometers. The height of the mercurial column in A C was noted, also the difference of the heights of mercury in the two columns A C, B D. From these data the absolute expansion of mercury can be computed; thus—

$$\frac{\text{excess of height of B D over A C}}{\text{height of A C}} = \text{absolute expansion.}$$

Of course, in arranging the experiment, means must be adopted for shutting off the heat of B D and its heater from the freezing mixture applied to A C. There would be also a tendency for a cold current to pass along the *lower* side of the tube from C to D, and for a warm current to pass along the *upper* side of it from D to C (Art. 45); but this is practically obviated by having the bore of the tube very small.

43. The absolute expansion of mercury when heated in a glass vessel being thus obtained, at various temperatures, it is clear that the difference between its absolute expansion at any temperature and its apparent expansion at the *same temperature* must be due to the cubical expansion of the glass

envelope. To find **the apparent expansion of mercury** when heated in a glass vessel, a glass cylinder is taken, to which is joined a bent capillary tube, as shown in Fig. 13. This is filled with mercury at 0° C., and the excess of its weight when filled over its weight when empty gives the precise weight of the mercury contained in the cylinder. When this is heated to a given temperature, a portion of the mercury is driven over into a small vessel placed to receive it. The weight of mercury thus expelled gives the difference between the weight of mercury required to fill the cylinder at 0° C. and that required to fill it at the given temperature.

Let the weight of the mercury, before the heating of the cylinder, be represented by W, and that of the mercury

Fig. 13.

expelled by w; then manifestly the weight of the mercury left in the cylinder is $W-w$.

But $w : W-w : :$ expansion of $w :$ expansion of $W-w$. And since the quantity $W-w$ contracts on cooling to zero, it must leave an empty space in the vessel; and this empty space at 0° C. must have the same ratio to the space occupied by $W-w$ as $w : W-w$; which represents the apparent expansion of the mercury, whose weight is $W-w$.

$$\therefore \frac{w}{W-w} = \text{apparent expansion of mercury in glass.}$$

If we divide the result by the number of degrees through which the temperature has been raised, we get the apparent expansion for 1°, or the *coefficient of apparent expansion*. Also by dividing the result obtained for any given temperature in Art. 42 by the difference of temperature of the two columns of mercury (Fig. 12), we get the *coefficient of absolute expansion* of mercury. And the difference between these coefficients is the coefficient of cubical expansion of glass.

44. The coefficient of absolute expansion of mercury for temperatures between 0° and 100° C. was found by Dulong and Petit to be $\frac{1}{5550}$; between 100° and 200° it is $\frac{1}{5425}$; and between 200° and 300° it is $\frac{1}{5300}$.

Also the coefficient of apparent expansion of mercury in glass was found by the same physicists to be $\frac{1}{6480}$.

$$\therefore \frac{1}{5550} - \frac{1}{6480} = \cdot 0000258.$$

= **coefficient of cubic expansion of glass**.

This added to the coefft. of apparent expansion of any liquid, when heated in a glass envelope, gives the coefft. of absolute expansion for that liquid.

45. Convection of Heat in Liquids.—It was noticed in Art. 29 (*e*) that when the lower strata of a body of air are heated an upward current is caused, the air rising from below as its density is diminished by expansion. The same thing occurs when the lower portion of a body of water or other liquid is heated; the lighter heated particles rise, while the heavier colder particles descend to take their place. This process is called 'convection.' It is the chief cause of both atmospheric and oceanic circulation. As a result of this law there is a general slow interchange of water between the equatorial and polar regions. As the water of the ocean in equatorial regions is expanded near the surface, it spreads northward and southward, while the colder water below takes its place. Thus there is a constant surface-motion from the equator to the poles, and a deep-sea motion in the opposite direction.

By the same law the influence of the 'Gulf Stream' is felt much farther than it would otherwise be. The origin of this great river within the Atlantic Ocean appears to be the 'head of water' formed in the Gulf of Mexico by the general westerly 'drift' across the Atlantic, which results from the Trade Winds blowing continually in that direction within the tropics. The impetus thus given being concentrated in the Gulf of Mexico, drives the current, which issues through the Strait of Florida, far into the open Atlantic. As fast, however, as it loses heat at the surface the warmer portions of the current rise, by the law of convection, to the surface, until at last the 'stream' spreads out in a thin layer and interdigitates with other surface currents.

Similarly in warming buildings by hot-water pipes.

46. Maximum Density of Water.—The general law of expansion on heating and contraction on cooling, which holds good for most liquids, is not found to apply *wholly* to water. Between the temperatures of 0° C. and 4° C. water behaves in an *exceptional manner; condensing*, between these limits, as its temperature rises, and *expanding* as its temperature falls from 4° C. to 0° C. This exceptional property of water is of immense importance in the economy of nature. The result is that the sp. gr. of ice is about ·92. This is why ice floats at the surface, and begins to form there, instead of at the bottom of the still water of our ponds and lakes. As the surface-water cools, it descends by the law of convection to the bottom ; and this kind of movement goes on until the whole mass of water is cooled to the temperature of 4° C. Below that temperature the surface-water expands until congelation sets in ; the great bulk, however, of deep water remaining at 4° C.

The temperature of maximum density (4° C.) may be shown by surrounding with a freezing-mixture a tall jar of water, into which two thermometers are inserted, one near the top, the other near the bottom. The colder heavier particles descend : the *lower* thermometer falls to 4° C., and remains stationary until the upper one falls to the same temperature. As cooling progresses further, the lighter colder particles rise, and the *upper* thermometer falls to 0° C. before the lower one.

As water is heated up to 100° C., its coefficient of expansion increases, as may be seen from the following volumes (by Despretz): 1 volume at 0° C. is at 20° C., 1·002 ; at 40° C., 1·008 ; at 60° C., 1·017 ; at 80° C., 1·029 ; at 100° C., 1·043.

47. The force with which water expands on freezing is very great. We see its effect in the bursting of water-pipes, producing leakage, which the next thaw discovers to us ; and it has been well shown by the experiments of Major Williams. Having filled a bomb-shell with water and closed it very tightly with a wooden plug, he exposed it to the severe cold of a Canadian winter: as the water was frozen it expelled the plug to a considerable distance. On another occasion the same gentleman closed a shell with an iron screw, and the expansive force of the freezing water was found sufficient to burst the shell. In nature this power is exhibited to an enormous extent. Fissures and joints in rocks, getting filled with water, are widened more and more at every severe frost, until at length often huge masses are forced off from the sea-cliff, or from the mountain-side; falling in the one case on the shore or into the sea, in the other case into valleys below, or upon glaciers. When these glaciers terminate in inland valleys, they deposit their burden in the form of terminal moraines; but in high northern latitudes, as on the Greenland coast, they often push their way out into the sea, where they are broken off by currents, and drifted away to more southern latitudes in the form of icebergs freighted with their rocky burden, until they melt and deposit these erratic blocks on the bed of the ocean. These causes, operating in past geological periods, have scattered many masses of rock far and wide from their original sources.

48. Heat and Work.—We have seen that, when bodies have their temperature raised, they, as a rule, expand. The force with which they do this is enormous, since it is equal to the pressure necessary to contract them to their original dimensions. A rod of wrought iron, for example, being heated from $0°$ C. to $100°$ C., increases $·0012$ of its original length (Art. 38). In doing so it will (if the bar be 1 inch square) lift a weight of 15 tons. This therefore represents the force required to make a square inch bar of iron $1·0012$ ft. long contract to 1 ft. If this weight were applied to the bar, the heat given off by the bar while contracting must be equal to that required to raise it from $0°$ C. to $100°$ C.

Here we see that *heat and work are mutually convertible.*

CHAPTER III.

CHANGES OF PHYSICAL CONDITION.

49. MATTER exists in three forms—solid, liquid, and gaseous (Art. 4). In solids the molecules are held together by a force called *molecular attraction*; but in gases this force is overcome, and the molecules are mutually repelled by the influence of heat. In a liquid these two forces seem to be pretty evenly balanced, there being just enough heat to alter the *state of aggregation* of the particles of the solid. Speaking generally solids may, by being sufficiently heated, be *liquefied*, and liquids *vaporised*; and by abstracting heat from them the contrary effect may be produced. Thus, at the normal pressure, water below 0° C. is a solid, between 0° C. and 100° C. a liquid, above 100° C. a vapour or gas. Some solids, however—as, for instance, carbon -- have never, by the greatest heat man has been able to produce, been turned in their simple form into either a liquid or a gas; while, on the other hand, the greatest cold known will not freeze alcohol.

We shall consider—

(1) Liquefaction of solids, or their conversion into liquids, together with the reverse process of solidification.

(2) Vaporisation of liquids, and the reverse process of liquefaction of gases and vapours.

LIQUEFACTION OF SOLIDS.

50. Speaking generally this change occurs when the heat that passes into a solid becomes sufficient to overcome mole-

cular attraction. Heat expended in liquefying a body is therefore converted into the work of severing the bond which, in the solid state, holds the molecules firmly together. It is clear, however, that in the liquid the intermolecular spaces must be somewhat greater than in the solid; consequently a solid body, on passing into the liquid condition, increases its volume. This is therefore **work** done by the heat which is used in melting a solid.

It follows that pressure ought to retard the liquefaction of solids; and this is found to be the case, except with ice and a few other solids,[1] which expand on solidifying, the melting of ice being *accelerated* by pressure. The freezing point is lowered by substances held in solution; and alloys fuse at a lower temperature than their ingredients. When particles of ice at 0° C. are pressed together, the pressure causes portions of them to melt at the points of contact, and they freeze together as soon as the pressure is removed. This is called **regelation**. By doubling the atmospheric pressure the melting-point of ice is lowered $\frac{1}{75}$th of a deg. F.

The power with which molecular attraction is capable of being exerted, being different for different kinds of matter, it follows that the temperature of liquefaction, or point of fusion, is not the same for all solids. Subjoined are a few of these points of fusion at 760 mm. pressure:—

Mercury .	−39° C.	Tin .	228° C.
Ice .	0° C.	Lead .	325° C.
Phosphorus .	44° C.	Silver .	1023° C.
Potassium .	58° C.	Gold .	1100° C.
Sodium .	98° C.	Iron .	1500° C.
Sulphur .	115° C.		

During the process of fusion, the heat that passes into

[1] Cast iron owes its suitability for casting to its expansion on solidifying. Bismuth and antimony also possess this property: the latter is used to counteract the effect of the contraction of lead in type-metal.

Laws of Fusion. Latent Heat.

the body is expended in the work of altering the state of aggregation of the molecules, so as to overcome the molecular attraction to which the rigidity of the solid is due. The temperature of the body therefore ceases to rise, until fusion is complete. The *effect of heat being thus sensibly lost*, thermal energy is said to become **latent** in the liquid.

51. Thus from theoretic considerations we may deduce the following **Laws of fusion** at constant pressure, which have been arrived at by processes of experiment and generalisation :—

(1) *The same substance always begins to melt at the same temperature.*

(2) *From the moment fusion begins till the moment at which it is completed the temperature of the body remains constant.*

52. *Definition.*—In speaking of quantities of heat it is necessary to have some unit of quantity, by reference to which they may be compared with one another. It is found convenient to adopt as a **thermal unit** *that quantity of heat which is sufficient to raise the temperature of one pound (or one gramme) of water* $1°$ C.[1]

Latent Heat of Water.—If one pound of water at $0°$ C. be mixed with one pound of water at $79°$ C., we get two pounds of water at $39·5°$ C. But if we dissolve one pound of ice in one pound of water at $79°$ C., we get two pounds of water at $0°$ C. It is clear, therefore, that the pound of warm water has, in melting the pound of ice, imparted to it as

---

[1] We have seen that the oxidising process of combustion is a source of heat (Art. 13). Subjoined are the heating powers of a few highly combustible substances :—

1 pound of hydrogen, when burnt, gives off 34,500 thermal units.

,,	marsh gas	,,	,,	13,000	,,	,,
,,	olive oil	,,	,,	9,860	,,	,,
,,	anthracite	,,	,,	8,460	,,	,,
,,	common coal	,,	,,	8,000	,,	,,
,,	coke	,,	,,	7,000	,,	,,

much thermal energy as would have raised a pound of water from 0° C. to 79° C.;

∴ latent heat of 1 pound of water = 79 thermal units.
or latent heat of water = 79° C. (= 142° F.).

53. Solution.—When a solid is dissolved in a liquid, the liquid parts with a portion of its own heat, until the quantity of heat thus imparted is just as much as will fuse an equal quantity of the solid in the dry state. When a solid is dissolved, therefore, in a liquid medium, there is always a *fall of temperature*[1] in the latter. As, however, it takes some time to equalise the temperature of a still liquid, solution proceeds but slowly, though faster in proportion as the quantity of heat in the liquid exceeds that required to melt the solid; also by stirring or shaking the particles of the solid are brought more quickly into contact with the warmer molecules of the liquid, and are consequently dissolved the sooner. The heat which disappears from the liquid assumes the form of latent heat in the substance dissolved. When a solid such as ice, which condenses during liquefaction, is dissolved in its own liquid, solution is hastened by a succession of warm particles of the liquid brought into contact with the solid by convection-currents.

Freezing-mixtures exemplify the latent heat of solution.

Parts by weight.

Sulphate of soda . 3 } lower temp. from +10° to −17°	
Dilute nitric acid . 2	
Pounded ice or snow 2 } ,, ,, +10° to −18°	
Common salt . . 1	

---

[1] We are discussing here the purely *physical* effects of solution. Of course when chemical combination takes place between the solid and the liquid, the heat engendered by this may more than compensate for the heat used in solution, and so mask the withdrawal of heat from the liquid. (See Arts. 13—16).

Solution. The Vitreous State.

In 'refrigerators,' or ice-making machines, the water to be frozen is placed in a metallic cylinder surrounded by a freezing-mixture.

As in solution a portion of heat becomes latent, so when the dissolved substance crystallises out from solution this heat is restored to the liquid. Water containing matter in solution (e.g. sea-water) does not freeze so readily as perfectly pure water does. When a body solidifies from solution, it generally assumes regular geometrical forms (crystals), of which we may take calcite and common salt as examples. This is called crystallising in the 'moist way;' when a body crystallises from a state of fusion, it is said to do so in the 'dry way.'

54. Some bodies pass through an intermediate stage on being converted from the liquid to the crystalline state. Glass is a typical example of this, its viscosity increasing till it becomes solid, and the intermediate state is therefore spoken of as the 'vitreous' state. It is found that if the siliceous materials of the glass are kept for a long time at a high temperature, and cooled slowly, they assume the crystalline state, and so lose their transparency.

These phenomena frequently occur in the igneous rocks of the earth's crust, which have been consolidated from a state of fusion at a very high temperature. In cases, however, where rapid cooling has occurred, the vitreous or glassy condition is assumed. The three most familiar instances of this are

Obsidian,	the glassy state of		trachyte,
Tachylite,	,,	,,	basalt,
Pitchstone,	,,	,,	felstone.

55. The phenomena exhibited by sulphur on solidifying are somewhat striking :—

(1) When molten sulphur is allowed to cool *slowly* it

crystallises in long, needle-shaped prisms at 115° C.

(2) When sulphur crystallises out at lower temperatures, from solution in carbon disulphide, it assumes the form of rhombic octohedra.

(3) When molten sulphur, heated to about 450° C., is *suddenly* cooled, it assumes the plastic state, with a consistency similar to that of caoutchouc, and retains this condition for several days, ultimately crystallising for the most part, however, in rhombic octohedra. There is a manifest analogy between this and the 'vitreous state.'

VAPORISATION.

56. We have seen that in a liquid the molecules are in constant motion among one another: The only impediment to the perfect freedom of their motion is a certain degree of cohesion, which liquids possess, as shown by hanging drops, and as the fusing-point is approached, this force becomes in many liquids considerable, producing the viscid state. Now, it must necessarily follow that in the course of their excursions some individual molecules reach the surface of the liquid; and not being encountered here by other molecules, they escape from the liquid into the air, through which their passage is much easier than it is through the liquid. In this way the atmosphere becomes charged with varying quantities of free molecules (water-vapour); and this process, by which the individual molecules of a liquid pass off into the air, is called **evaporation**.

Again, when heat is applied to the exterior of a vessel containing water at 100° C., portions of the liquid contiguous

Conditions Favourable to Evaporation.

to the heated parts of the vessel are rapidly converted into steam, which rises through the liquid, throwing the liquid into commotion. This phenomenon is boiling, or **ebullition.** We shall consider these separately.

I. EVAPORATION.

57. As in a liquid the energy of motion among the molecules is due to the heat latent in the liquid, so by adding more and more heat to a liquid the energy of its molecular motion may be increased.

The higher the temperature of a liquid, therefore, the greater the number of molecules which reach a given unit of surface in a given unit of time (say, the number which reach a *square inch* of surface in a *second*), and pass off into the atmosphere.

> The first condition upon which rapidity of evaporation depends is therefore **temperature.**

If now the temperature remain constant, and the liquid which has been contained in a deep vessel be poured into a shallow one, the number of square units of surface is thereby increased. And since the same number of molecules will escape from each unit of surface, the aggregate evaporation in a given time is proportionately increased.

> The second condition upon which the rapidity of evaporation depends is the **extent of surface exposed to the air.**

Further, it is manifest that the freer the air in contact with the liquid is from water-vapour, the more readily will the molecules of the latter escape into it. And since there is a limit to the absorptive capacity of the air ('saturation'), a point is reached at which the molecules suspended in the air are precipitated by entanglement in the liquid, as fast as those of the liquid escape into it.

The third condition may, then, be stated thus: evaporation is retarded according to the degree of the **saturation of the adjacent air.**

By removal of air from the surface of the liquid as fast as it approaches saturation, and supplying its place with drier air, it follows from the third condition that evaporation is accelerated. This explains the drying effect of a **wind**.

58. As liquids exist at the ordinary temperature of the air, they are removed of course, some more, some less, from their boiling-points. Those which, at the ordinary temperature, are nearest their boiling-points, possess their molecules in a greater rapidity of motion, and therefore evaporate more rapidly. Such liquids are said to be 'volatile.' Of these ether may be taken as an example of an extremely volatile liquid. Owing to this property, coupled with its inflammability, its vapour may be ignited at a considerable distance from the surface of the liquid. Carbon disulphide is another example of an extremely volatile liquid. Water is but moderately volatile as compared with these. Alcohol is more volatile than water, but less so than the other two. On the other hand, in some dense oily liquids—such, e.g., as oil of vitriol—the molecular motion must be extremely sluggish. The tension of this liquid as its temperature rises towards the boiling-point (Art. 72) becomes so great, that its distillation in a glass retort is a dangerous operation, unless special precautions are adopted.

Strictly speaking, a substance exists in the state of **vapour** only so long as the individual molecules are moving freely and separately; as soon as they collect into minute vesicles or spherules of water and so become visible, they form **cloud**. When a cloud is distributed among dry air the little drops of water disappear again by evaporation, and the cloud is lost to the sight; a phenomenon that may be observed as the cloud of condensed steam from a locomotive vanishes.

59. It must be borne in mind that the pressure of the

Elasticity of Vapours.

atmosphere (fifteen pounds nearly to the square inch) retards the escape of molecules from the surface of a liquid; and this resistance diminishes as the atmospheric **pressure** is withdrawn. This may be shown by the increased evaporation of water under the receiver of an air-pump, as the internal pressure is lessened. And, *à fortiori*, if the atmospheric pressure be withdrawn entirely, the rapidity of evaporation reaches a maximum, and becomes practically instantaneous. When, however, the vacuum has received so much vapour that the elasticity of the vapour enables it to exert a pressure upon the surface of the liquid with a force equal to that with which the molecules escape from the surface, evaporation is practically arrested, and the space is said to be 'saturated' with vapour. When a very volatile liquid, such as ether, is placed under the receiver, and the air partly withdrawn, the elasticity of its vapour causes it to escape so violently from the liquid as to produce the phenomenon of ebullition. Liquids in general are found to boil *in vacuo* at from $33°$ to $77°$ C. below their boiling-points at 760 mm. pressure.

60. From the above considerations (Art. 59) we may deduce the following **Laws of Evaporation**:—

    (1) *All volatile liquids tend to pass into vapour, and do so very rapidly in a vacuum.*

    (2) *The vapours of different liquids have, at the same temperature, different elastic forces.*

These laws may be illustrated by an experiment represented in Fig. 14. Four glass tubes, rather more than 30 in. long (barometer tubes), are taken. Being filled with mercury, they are then inverted and the open ends plunged beneath mercury contained in a trough. At the ordinary pressure of the air the mercury sinks in each tube to the level of about 30 inches above the surface. Now if into tube *b* a drop of water, into *c* a drop of alcohol, and into *d* a drop of ether be passed, each of these liquids will rise through the column of mercury, and on reaching the vacuum, be instantly converted into vapour. In each case the vapour by its elastic force pushes the mercury down; but further in the case of alcohol than in that of water, and much further still in the case of ether.

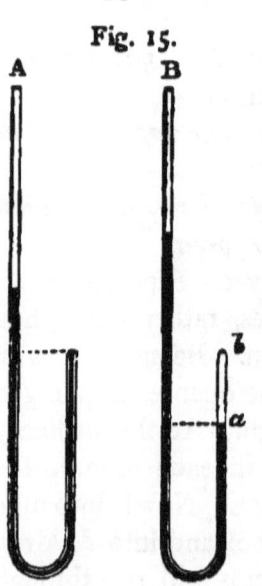

Fig. 14.

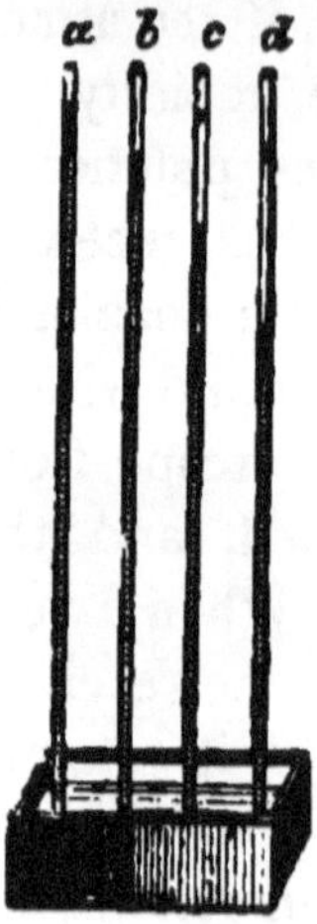

Fig. 15.

61. As the vapours of different liquids have, at the same temperature, different elastic forces, so the elastic force of any given vapour increases with its temperature, as is the case with gases. (See Note I.) This may be illustrated by taking a bent tube closed at the end of the shorter arm, and partly filled with mercury, as at A, Fig. 15. If then a few drops of ether be passed into the shorter arm, and the tube be plunged into a water-bath at a temperature somewhat above the boiling-point of ether, the mercury sinks in the shorter arm and rises in the longer, as at B; while the space $a\,b$ is filled with a vapour, that has all the appearance of a gas. If the water be gradually cooled, this gas (which is the superheated vapour of ether) is liquefied. In fact, the distinction between a 'gas' and a 'vapour' is not based on any true physical distinction; they are merely convenient terms to denote—the first, an aëriform body existing at a temperature somewhat above its boiling-point; the second, an aëriform body at a temperature not exceeding its boiling-point. **Superheated steam** is therefore as much a gas as carbonic acid, which can be liquefied by sufficient cold and pressure. We must, in studying the phenomena of evaporation, guard against the error of supposing that there is an abrupt change from the liquid to the aëriform state, or *vice versâ*. As Andrews has shown, 'the

gaseous and liquid states are only distant stages of the same condition of matter, and are capable of passing into one another by a process of continuous change.' Carbon dioxide, when subjected to a pressure of 40 atmospheres, is partly liquefied. If it is still further compressed (the temperature remaining unaltered) more of the gas is liquefied. If, however, the temperature is raised, the tension of the gas is increased. And by simultaneously increasing both pressure and temperature, the dense gas becomes more and more like a liquid, and the light liquid more and more like a gas, until at temperature 30·9° C. and pressure equal to about 74 atmospheres, the distinction between them vanishes, and the **critical point** is reached.

62. **Liquefaction of Gases.**—*Sulphur dioxide*, the gaseous product of the combustion of sulphur in air, can be easily liquefied. It is not found to obey Boyle's Law (Art. 26) below about $+$ 30° C., and this would suggest that at 0° C. we are near the temperature of liquefaction of this gas. This is found to be the case, for on passing dry sulphur dioxide into a bent tube embedded in a mixture of common salt and pounded ice (Art. 53), a quantity of the substance may be obtained in the liquid state. Its boiling point is $-$ 8° C. Its evaporation is so rapid that it supplies a very powerful means for the production of cold; *e.g.* if the liquid be poured upon the bulb of an ordinary thermometer wrapped in cotton-wool, the temperature often sinks to $-$ 50° C. in a warm room, and the mercury is frozen. A more general idea of the relation which the physical state bears to pressure and temperature may be got from the following table, compared with Art. 72 :—

Gas.	Boiling-point at 1 atm.	Coërcible by pressure of
Sulphur dioxide (SO_2)	$-$ 8° C.	2 atm. at $+$ 15° C.
Chlorine (Cl_2)	} $-$ 34° C.	6 atm. at 0° C.
Ammonia (H_3N)		
Sulphuretted hydrogen (H_2S)	$-$ 62° C.	16 atm. at $+$ 15° C.
Carbon dioxide (CO_2)	$-$78·2° C.	36 atm. at $+$ 15° C.
Nitrous oxide (N_2O)	$-$ 90° C.	30 atm. at 0° C.
Hydrochloric acid (HCl)	.	40 atm. at $+$ 10° C.

The above results have been known for some time, in some instances for half a century; Faraday being especially distinguished as one of the first and most successful workers in this line. He obtained his results in strong, bent, sealed glass tubes. One end of the tube held the materials from which the gas was generated, while the other served as a condenser, and was embedded in a powerfully frigorific mixture. (Art. 68.)

Towards the close of the year 1877 a great advance was made by M. Cailletet, of Chatillons-sur-Seine. The first decided results were obtained by means of a powerful hydraulic press acting upon a bed of mercury contained in a powerful steel cylinder, and communicating with a glass cylinder of small diameter, containing the gas to be liquefied. Of the three gaseous hydro-carbons *Acetylene*, *Ethylene*, and *Ethyle Hydride* (which in equal volumes have, with the same weight of carbon, hydrogen in the proportions of 1 : 2 : 3), the second had been found by Faraday to be coërcible at about 0° C. by 44 atm. Acetylene was first liquefied by M. Cailletet at a pressure rather greater, and then Ethyle Hydride at a pressure rather less, than that required for the liquefaction of Acetylene. *Methyle Hydride* ('Marsh-gas') and *Nitric Oxide* (N_2O_2) were liquefied soon afterwards. The remaining gases presented greater difficulties. Both *Oxygen* and *Carbon monoxide*, when brought to a temperature of − 29° C. by means of liquid sulphur dioxide at a pressure of 300 atm., maintain the gaseous state. But if either of them is then suddenly distended (comp. Art. 31) so as to reduce the temperature some 200° more, an *intense mist* immediately appears, produced by the liquefaction (perhaps by the solidification) of the oxygen or of the carbon monoxide. (Comp. Art. 68.) This phenomenon is observed from the distension of the mon- and di-oxides of carbon, and of nitrous and nitric oxides. A similar mist is produced in the case of oxygen even when the gas is at the ordinary temperature, provided time is

Freezing by Evaporation. 53

allowed for it to lose the heat acquired by the simple fact of compression. (Art. 8.) *Nitrogen* pure and dry compressed at about 200 atm. at the temperature of $+ 13°$ C., then suddenly distended, is condensed in the clearest manner, in the first instance into drops of appreciable volume. After these experiments the liquefaction of *Air* followed naturally. *Hydrogen* was condensed with greater difficulty, but undoubted results were obtained and well attested. 'On operating with pure hydrogen compressed at 280 atm. then abruptly distended, a mist exceedingly fine and subtile was seen to form through the whole length of the gas, and to suddenly disappear.'[1]

M. Pictet, of Geneva, working independently of M. Cailletet, obtained even more marked results. The apparatus used by the latter is remarkable for its simplicity;[2] the former, using more elaborate arrangements, and previously cooling the gases operated upon, by powerful frigorific mixtures, has obtained in the liquid state considerable quantities of the gases previously reputed incoërcible. M. Cailletet has found that the *critical point* (Art. 61) of all these gases is below $- 90°$ C., since at that temperature a pressure of 370 atm. fails to liquefy them.

63. Since heat is expended in converting a liquid into a vapour, becoming *latent* in the vapour, it follows that conditions which greatly accelerate evaporation are favourable to the production of cold. On this principle **Carré's Freezing Machine** is constructed. An extremely volatile substance (ammonia) is chosen for the purpose; and by a sudden withdrawal of pressure from liquid ammonia a very low temperature is obtained by rapid evaporation.

The machine consists essentially of two strong wrought-iron or copper vessels, the boiler b, and the condenser c, Fig. 16. The communication between these is maintained by the pipe d. The cylinder a can be removed from a corre-

---

[1] *Comptes Rendus*, le 31 Déc. 1877.
[2] *Nature*, Jan. 31, 1878.

sponding cylinder which forms a portion of the condenser. At *e* is a small vessel containing water, and furnished with a screw, by loosening which all the air in the machine is allowed to

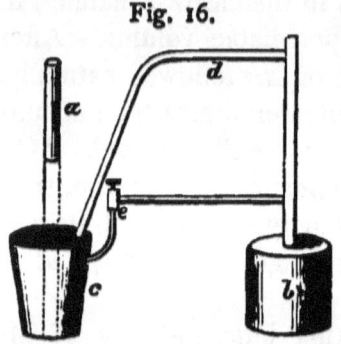
Fig. 16.

escape when heated, while the water in *e* absorbs any ammonia suspended in the air which escapes. The boiler *b* is nearly filled with a strong solution of ammonia, and heated, while the condenser *c* is kept cool, by being immersed in a stream of cold water. The ammonia, *being driven off in the gaseous state* by heat, passes into *c*, where by cold and pressure combined it is *liquefied*. A stream of cold water is next made to pass over *b*, while the cylinder *a*, filled with the liquid to be frozen, is inverted in the condenser. The pressure inside being suddenly removed, the liquid ammonia in *c* evaporates so rapidly that the cold produced freezes the contents of the cylinder.

64. The same law is shown by the **cryophorus**, which in its simplest form consists of two glass bulbs connected by a tube. One of these is partly filled with water, and all the air expelled by boiling, after which the aperture is sealed. If then all the water be driven into one bulb, and the *other bulb* embedded in ice, the water will evaporate so rapidly as soon to freeze the residue.

A similar phenomenon is the freezing of water under the receiver of an air-pump, when placed over a tray of oil of vitriol, which absorbs the vapour as fast as it comes off.

When a hot and a cold vessel, both containing a liquid, communicate by a tube, the pressure in both is *that of the cold vessel*. This principle is applied in Watt's **Condenser** in the steam-engine.

65. The ocean, rivers, &c., and moist ground, are constantly parting with vapour at their surface. This is held in suspension by the air, within a certain limit, which

Hygrometry.

varies with the temperature, air being able to hold in suspension more at higher temperatures than at lower temperatures. When the air is so far charged with vapour as to be unable to absorb more, it is said to be **saturated**. If then the air be cooled it will deposit some of its vapour in the form of dew. The temperature at which the air begins to deposit moisture is called the **dewpoint**. The degree of saturation of the air is its **hygrometric state**, and instruments by which this is ascertained are called **hygrometers**. One of the commonest of these is the *wet-bulb hygrometer*.

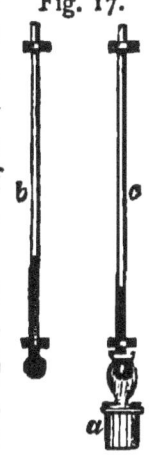

Fig. 17.

The principle of this instrument may be understood by reference to Fig. 17, which represents two thermometers, the bulb of one (*c*) having a piece of muslin wrapped round it. This dips into a vessel of water *a*, and the water passes up by capillary attraction between the fibres of the muslin. So long as the air is not saturated, evaporation will go on at the surface of the muslin, and consequently the mercury in *c* will stand at a lower level than in *b*. When the air is *saturated* the evaporation ceases, and the mercury stands at the *same level in both tubes*, indicating that the *dewpoint* is reached, and we may expect rain. On the other hand, the greater the difference between the heights of the two columns of mercury, the drier the air. (Comp. Art. 109.)

Fig. 18.

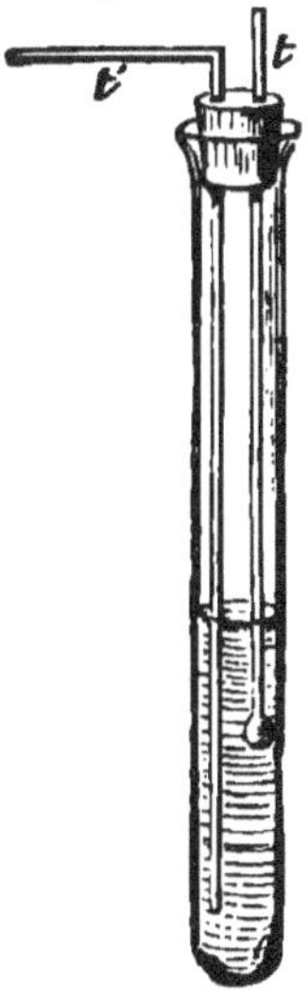

66. Two other forms of the hygrometer are those invented by Daniell and by Regnault, in both of which the cold produced by evaporation of ether is turned to account.

The principle of Regnault's may be understood by reference to Fig. 18 which represents a large test tube, partly filled with ether, and furnished with a loosely fitting cork, through which are passed a thermometer t, and a bent tube t', both reaching down into the liquid. If now air be blown through t' it will rise in bubbles through the ether, and accelerate its evaporation, producing a corresponding loss of heat on the part of the liquid. When this is cooled down to a certain point, moisture will be deposited on the outside of the tube in the form of dew, and the thermometer t will show the temperature of the ether at the instant, which is therefore the *dewpoint* of the air. By comparing this with a thermometer exposed to the air, we can find how many degrees the temperature is above the dewpoint.

In actual operation the apparatus represented in the last figure is attached by a tube to an aspirator, the cork being made air-tight. By this means a current of air is drawn through the ether, while the cooling effects of evaporation are not interfered with by the proximity of the warm body of the observer.

67. By making a current of air pass very rapidly through a body of ether by blowing into it with a pair of bellows, and immersing a tube of water in the ether, ice may be formed in a very short time even in a warm room. This shows why a *warm* wind cools the skin, and why 'ether spray' locally destroys sensation.

68. **Solidification of Carbonic Anhydride.**—For this purpose a large quantity of the gas must be generated in a very confined space. A strong wrought-iron tube, capable of resisting a pressure of at least 40 atmospheres, is furnished with a screw stop-cock of great strength. In the bottom of the tube is placed a quantity of bicarbonate of soda. A small cylindrical jar containing oil of vitriol is passed steadily into the tube, which is then securely closed. On shaking the apparatus the acid is spilt upon the carbonate, and decomposes it. Carbonic anhydride is set free in abundance, and by pressure is partly liquefied. When the screw-tap is loosened, the cold produced by excessive

Latent Heat of Vapours.

expansion (Art. 31) is so great that the gas is partly frozen, and is crystallised into a spray of carbonic anhydride snow. This snow may be collected in considerable quantity, and, being mixed with ether, forms *one of the most powerful freezing agents known*. Faraday obtained by it a temperature of $-110°$ C., the alcohol in the thermometer used to estimate the temperature being itself reduced to the consistence of oil. At this temperature nitrous oxide and some other gases are converted into clear, transparent ice.

69. Since water-vapour is continually passing off from the lungs in respiration, and from the skin by perspiration (either 'sensible' or 'insensible'), it follows that the atmosphere of a warm inhabited room contains a large quantity of such vapour suspended in it. This is at once shown to be the case, when a bottle of cold water or wine from the cellar is brought into the room. The temperature of the air in immediate proximity to the cold vessel falls below the dew-point of the room, and a deposit of dew takes place on the surface of the vessel.

70. When water-vapour suspended in the atmosphere is condensed, the **latent heat** of the vapour (which is very considerable) is given back to the atmosphere. In this way the thermal effect of the Gulf Stream is felt much farther inland than it would otherwise be, since the vapour given off from its surface is borne by diffusion and by winds over the land, and on precipitation gives up its latent heat. The severity of an English, as compared with a Canadian, winter is thus greatly mitigated.

71. When the globules of water in the state of 'cloud' collect into large groups in their descent through the air, we get *Rain*. When rain is frozen in its downward passage we get *Hail*. When the water-vapour is suddenly cooled below the freezing-point, we get clusters of minute crystals called *Snow*. Snow is really a *sublimate* of water-vapour, though this term is generally confined in its appli-

cation to such substances (e.g. arsenic) as condense ordinarily on a cold surface immediately into the solid state. In the production of *flowers of sulphur*, the natural process, whereby snow is produced, is imitated artificially. Native sulphur is evaporated in a large crucible within a furnace, and the vapours are conducted into chambers outside the furnace, which are kept at a temperature considerably below the melting (or freezing) point of sulphur. In these cool chambers the vapour is sublimated in the form of very fine crystals (flowers of sulphur.)

II. EBULLITION.

72. We have seen that, when a liquid is subjected to the influence of heat, three results follow:—

(1) The liquid expands slightly.
(2) Its temperature rises.
(3) Evaporation from its surface is accelerated.

These results go on simultaneously up to a certain point, which varies for different liquids. As the temperature approaches this point, globules of steam are produced in the lower regions of the liquid, contiguous to the heated walls of the vessel, and rise towards the surface; but in doing so they pass through the cooler layers of liquid above, and, parting with some of their heat, collapse. This is the phenomenon known as **simmering**. As the warmer particles of water ascend from below, the cooler particles descend to take their place, so that circulation by convection is established in the liquid. Soon, however, the temperature of the whole body of the liquid becomes equalised; then the steam generated at the bottom rises through the liquid without being condensed, and escapes at the surface. This is **ebullition**. It will be easy to see that this phenomenon can only come about when the elastic force of the vapour formed within the liquid is sufficiently great to *lift the atmospheric pressure* upon its surface. In the case of very volatile liquids, as ether and alcohol, the great elasticity of the vapour comes in to aid the expansive energy imparted by heat; water, being less volatile, requires more heat than these to make it boil, or, in other words, to enable its vapour to lift the atmospheric pressure (= 15 pounds to the square inch); denser and less mobile liquids, have still higher boiling-points. These conclusions from the theory of heat are confirmed by experiment.

Table of boiling-points at a pressure of 760 mm.

Sulphur dioxide .	−8° C.	Turpentine . .	160° C.
Chloride of ethyl	11° C.	Concentrated sul-	
Ether	35° C.	phuric acid . .	327° C.
Alcohol . . .	78° C.	Mercury . . .	350° C.
Distilled water .	100° C.	Sulphur	490° C.

73. Here we see a general law of rise of boiling-points in inverse ratio to the elasticity of the vapour of liquids. But it can be demonstrated by experiment that ebullition depends upon the tension of the vapour of the liquid being able to overcome atmospheric pressure. Let us take the case of water.

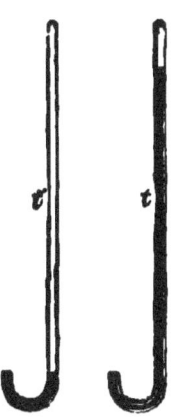

Fig. 19.

In Fig. 19, *t* represents a barometer-tube, into the vacuum of which a few drops of water are introduced. If then the long arm be enclosed in another tube, which communicates with a vessel in which water is heated, the water-vapour in t will gradually expand as the temperature rises, and force the mercury down. When the water boils, the mercury is found to stand at the same level in both arms, as shown in t'; and this indicates *equality of pressure within and without the tube.* (See Note I. p. 97.)

When a bubble of steam forms near the bottom of a vessel of water, its expansive force has to overcome the resistance due to pressure of atmosphere + weight of column of water above the bubble. As it rises higher, the latter quantity diminishes, and, when the bubble reaches the surface, vanishes. As the bubble is relieved from pressure, it of course expands, and in doing so suffers a slight fall of temperature; the temperature of steam in the lower layers of the water is consequently higher than at the surface. This is one reason why, in obtaining the boiling-point of the thermometer, the tube was immersed in steam, and not in boiling water. (Art. 19.)

74. The variation of boiling-point with pressure is further illustrated by its gradual sinking, as we ascend a mountain; so that on the summit of Mont Blanc, for instance, it would not be easy to make good tea or to boil eggs. The lowering of the boiling-point as we ascend occurs to the extent of about $1°$ C. for every 1,000 feet. To counteract the effects of the diminution of atmospheric pressure, and consequent lowering of the temperature of ebullition in high altitudes, and to heat water sufficiently for culinary purposes, M. Papin adopted the plan of substituting artificial for natural pressure. Papin's **digester** is a boiler fitted with an air-tight lid, and furnished with a valve attached to a weighted lever, by which the internal pressure is indicated, on the principle of the steel-yard. The steam being thus confined, reacts upon the surface of the water, and raises the boiling-point accordingly. The digester is extensively used in the arts for the purpose of heating water to a higher temperature

Latent Heat of Steam. 61

than 100° C., and thereby increasing its solvent power for organic substances.

This law of the elevation of boiling-point by increase of pressure bears important relation to the application of steam to mechanical purposes. Suppose the area of the piston of a steam-engine to be equal to one square foot (= 144 sq. inches). Then the resistance which the tension of the steam in the boiler is able to overcome will be just equal to the pressure of the atmosphere ($=15 \times 144 = 2160$ pounds to the square foot) so long as the temperature of the water is 100° C.

As soon as the resistance to be overcome (in other words, the work to be done) by the steam is increased beyond this quantity, the piston, cylinder, and boiler are converted into a *digester*, and the temperature of the water and of the steam (which have the same temperature) rises until the expansive force of the steam becomes sufficient to overcome the resistance either of the loaded piston or of the walls of the boiler. The temperature, therefore, of steam in high-pressure engines is always considerably above 100° C.

75. The fall of the boiling-point with diminution of pressure may be illustrated by a simple experiment. Take a good-sized flask half-filled with water, and boil this for a few minutes until the air is all expelled by the steam. The flask being then closed with a good cork, and inverted, the tension of the steam in the interior may be reduced by throwing cold water from a sponge upon the flask. The tension of the steam instantly becomes less than that of the vapour in the hot water, and ebullition is reproduced at a lower temperature than 100° C.

76. When water boils, the heat that passes into it is *partly converted into work*—the work of lifting the atmosphere, if ebullition takes place in an open vessel; the work of driving machinery, propelling a steamship, or drawing a railway train, if the steam is generated within the boiler of an engine. The rest of the heat is used up in warming the

engine or the vessel in which ebullition goes on. The temperature remains constant so long as the pressure does so, every increment of heat becoming latent in the additional steam. Judging from the work done and the amount of heat dissipated, we should conclude the **latent heat of steam** to be very great. It may be computed thus: Water being made to boil, the steam from it is conducted by a tube to the bottom of a vessel containing ice-cold water. In this the steam is at once condensed, parting with its latent heat to the cold water, the temperature of which rises until it begins to boil.

If the receiver has been well protected, so as to prevent the escape of heat from its sides, it is found that for every 5·36 pounds of cold water we get 6·36 pounds of boiling water; $\therefore$ the latent heat of 1 pound of steam (given up during its condensation into water) is sufficient to raise 5·36 pounds of water from 0° C. to 100° C.

Since a thermal unit = heat required to raise one pound of water one degree, the heat required to raise 5·36 pounds one degree = 5·36 thermal units, and 100 times as much is of course required to raise the like quantity of water through 100° C.;

$\therefore$ latent heat of 1 pound of steam = 536 thermal units;
or, latent heat of steam = 536° C.

77. We are now prepared to formulate the general **laws of Ebullition**:—

(1) *The same liquid always boils at the same temperature, if the pressure be the same.*

(2) *However great the heat to which a liquid is exposed, from the moment ebullition commences the temperature ceases to rise.*

(3) *Tension of steam = pressure of external air.*

78. It is clear that the presence of air in water must—on account of the excess of its coefficient of expansion over that of water (Art. 27)—facilitate ebullition. Nitrogen

and Oxygen are both slightly soluble in water, and Carbon dioxide more so ; it follows, therefore, that ordinary water contains these gases in solution. By boiling water for some time, so as to expel the air, and allowing it to cool while kept quite motionless, the boiling-point afterwards is affected very considerably. Such **non-aërated water** may be raised to a temperature of 130° or 140° C. before ebullition sets in.

The boiling-point is also raised by the presence of **solid matter** held in solution in the water; and is sometimes slightly affected by the **material** of the vessel in which it is heated, another reason for not allowing the bulb to dip into the water, in finding the boiling-point of a thermometer. The temperature of the steam which comes off is not affected by the nature of the vessel. (Art. 19 and 73.)

79. The purest water is obtained by **distillation**, which consists in boiling and recondensing the water, by passing the steam through a cold tube. The non-volatile matters (if any) contained in the water are left behind in the boiler. The apparatus is commonly known as a 'still.'

80. We must not omit to notice the power of heat to effect **chemical dissociation** in numerous instances. Ex. gr. :—

Mercuric oxide, *heated*, splits up into mercury and oxygen.
Ammonium nitrate, 	„ 	„ 	nitrous oxide and water.
Potassium chlorate, 	„ 	„ 	potassium chloride and oxygen.
Limestone, 	„ 	„ 	lime and carbon dioxide.

The subject belongs to Chemistry, and cannot be treated more fully here, but the above are a few among the many instances of this important function of heat.

In every such instance heat is expended in setting free substances (e.g. oxygen and carbon dioxide); but the **work** thus done is not lost, for it is converted back again into heat, when these bodies enter into new combinations. (Art. 16.)

Ebullition.

81. Problem.—*To find the volume of steam produced by a given weight of water at 4° C.*

The weight of a litre of dry air at 0° C. is known to be 1·2932 grammes.

∴ weight of 1 litre of air at 100° C. $= 1\cdot 2932 \times \dfrac{273}{373}$ grammes.

Also the vapour density of steam is known to be ·622.

∴ weight of 1 litre of steam $= \dfrac{1\cdot 2932 \times 273 \times \cdot 622}{373}$ grammes;

and (since 1 litre = 1000 ccm)

weight of 1 ccm of steam $= \dfrac{1\cdot 2932 \times 273 \times \cdot 622}{373 \times 1000} = \dfrac{1}{1698}$ grm.

∴ $\dfrac{1}{1698}$ gramme of water at 4° C. produces 1 ccm of steam; and 1 gramme of water at 4° C. produces 1698 ccm of steam.

∴ x grammes of water at 4° C. give 1698 x ccm of steam.

Corollary.—Since 1 grm. of water at 4° C. fills 1 ccm, it follows that the volume of steam at 100° C., produced by a given quantity of water, is about 1700 times the *volume* which that water occupies at 4° C.

82. This result helps us to understand the immense power of steam generated rapidly in a confined space—a power which is manifested by the disastrous results that oftentimes accompany the bursting of engine-boilers.

In nature it is exhibited on a far grander scale in the phenomena connected with volcanic eruptions.

CHAPTER IV.

CONDUCTION OF HEAT.

83. WHEN heat is transmitted through a body—as, for instance, a bar of metal—by each particle giving up some of its heat to adjacent particles that have less heat, the process is called **conduction**, and the material through which it passes is called a *conductor*. In *fluid* substances, this process is facilitated by *convection* (Art. 45), the more highly heated particles being distributed among the cooler ones.

Bodies through which heat travels best are said to be *good* conductors; such are most of the metals : other bodies are said to be *bad* conductors; such as resin, glass, wood, woollen fabrics, furs, and especially liquids and aëriform fluids. The flow of heat along a poker, when one end is thrust into the fire, or along the handle of a silver spoon, the bowl of which is immersed in a hot fluid, are instances of conduction. A handkerchief wrapped tightly round a polished ball of metal may be held some time in a candle flame without taking fire, the heat passing so rapidly into the metal that the temperature of the cloth remains below that which is necessary for ignition. Good conductors take up heat and give it off rapidly, as a result of which the variations of the temperature of the land are much greater than those of the ocean. So the sensation of heat or cold from a metallic bar is much keener than that from wood or woollen cloth of the same temperature. Thus a bar of cold iron, or even a bath of mercury, at a temperature of $5°C.$, would feel colder than water at the same temperature. In either case the sensation of cold arises from the hand parting with heat to the particles in immediate contact with it; while the heat taken up by these particles is passed on to other particles much more quickly in the cold metal than in the cold water.

84. As heat travels along a solid body, such as a bar of metal, some of it is given off from the surface particles to surrounding bodies. So long as the heat supplied from one end exceeds that which is given off from the surface of the bar, its temperature goes on rising; the temperature of any point being more or less, according as it is near or remote from the source of heat: this is the **variable stage** of conduction, during which the rapidity of the flow depends upon the difference of temperature. After a time the temperature of each portion of the bar remains constant, and it gives off as much heat as it receives: this is the **permanent stage** of conduction.

Now, since the capacity of bodies for heat varies considerably (see Chap. V.), the specific heat may mask the conductivity of a body while the variable stage lasts. We cannot, therefore, estimate the relative conductive powers of different substances except in the permanent stage.

The following have been found to be the **relative conducting powers** of the commoner metals by heating at one end a bar of each metal until the 'permanent stage' is reached, the distant end being of course at the temperature of the surrounding air. The temperatures of equidistant points on the bar are then estimated by thermometers or by the thermo-pile.

Silver . . . 100	Steel . . . 12
Copper . . . 77·6	Iron . . . 11·9
Gold . . . 53·2	Lead . . . 8·5
Brass . . . 33	Platinum . . . 8·2
Zinc . . . 19·9	Bismuth . . . 1·9
Tin . . . 14·5	

Relative Conductivities.

85. The difference in the conductivities of different metals may be illustrated as follows :—

Fig. 20 represents a bar of copper and a similar bar of iron, joined at one end. On each bar, at the same distance from the joint, is a small piece of phosphorus, p, p'. If a lamp be applied at the point of junction, the heat is conducted along both bars, but along the copper bar much faster than along the iron, as is shown by the phosphorus at

Fig. 20.

p taking fire some time before that at p', indicating a temperature of nearly 60° C. at the spot p.

Fig. 21 represents two similar bars, to the under surface of each of which a series of corks is affixed by means of white wax. When this is melted the corks fall. On heating the centre by a lamp, we find that several corks drop from

Fig. 21.

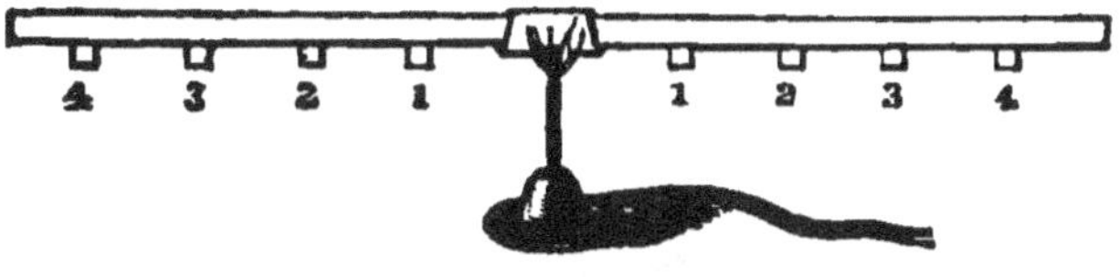

the copper bar before any fall from the iron bar, on account of the more rapid passage of heat through the copper.

The same property for different metals may be shown by the apparatus invented by Ingenhousz. In this rods of different materials coated with wax are inserted by means of corks in tubulures so that their ends terminate inside a vessel of hot water, and the relative conductivities are estimated from the extent to which the wax is melted.

86. *Applications of the conduction and non-conduction of Heat.*

(1) By packing in bran, sawdust, &c., ice may be kept some time from melting, and liquids may be kept warm.

(2) Double walls and windows are a great protection from severity of weather, on account of the air enclosed between them. For the same reason a loose coat is warmer than a tightly fitting one of the same material.

(3) Red-hot iron may be held in the hand, protected by a thin layer of asbestos, which is a very poor conductor.

(4) Red-hot cannon balls can be wheeled to the gun's mouth in wooden barrows filled with sand.

(5) Woollen cloth, furs, &c., contain air between the fibres, and this being a bad conductor prevents the heat of the body from escaping.

(6) The small conductive power of burnt *fire-clay* makes it very useful for lining fire-grates and stoves. The fire-bricks prevent heat from escaping into and through the wall at the back; while they retain the heat, and give off almost as much as the front of the fire does.

(7) Fibrous substances conduct heat much more in the direction of their fibres than transversely. Hence heat passes up and down the trunk of a tree much more readily than it passes outwards. This law, coupled with the law that liquids can be reduced to a much lower temperature without freezing when contained in capillary tubes, protects the tree from frost, and enables it to resist the inclemency of the winter season. Moreover, in the bark the tree has a sheathing of much less conductive power than the wood.

87. The conductivity of iron wire is beautifully shown by a very simple experiment. A piece of ordinary wire gauze is taken, and lowered in a horizontal position into a candle or gas flame (Fig. 22). The flame continues to burn only below the gauze, though a quantity of the gas escapes unburnt through the meshes, since if the gauze be lowered into the region of non-combustion [Fig. 2 (1)] the gas may be kindled by applying a light above.

Or we may vary the experiment thus: instead of lowering

Fig. 22.

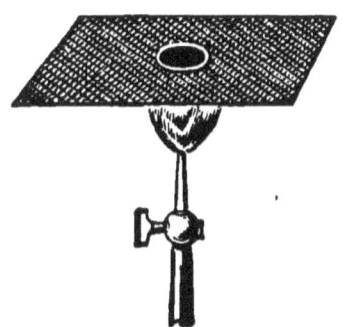

the gauze into a flame, we place it horizontally about an inch above the nozzle of a common gas-burner. The gas being allowed to escape, rises through the gauze, and if a light is

Fig. 23.

applied above, a flame is produced on the upper side of the gauze, not communicating with the nozzle (Fig. 23). In each case the high conductive power of the iron wire enables it to convey away so much heat from the region of the flame that the temperature is reduced below that which is required for kindling the gas on the other side.

88. The **Safety-lamp** is constructed on this principle. Its object is to guard against explosions in mines, which are often of a very terrible nature. They arise from the presence of light carburetted hydrogen ('marsh gas'), which, when mixed with twice its own volume of oxygen or about ten times its own volume of air, explodes with great violence on the application of a light, from the instantaneous formation of a large quantity of steam and carbon dioxide. Mere hot iron wire will not cause explosion; and we have seen that a fine wire-gauze is capable of shutting off completely the flame of a combustible gas (e.g. coal-gas, of which marsh gas is a principal constituent), so as to prevent it from igniting the same gas on the other side of the gauze. When, therefore, an ordinary oil lamp completely surrounded by a cylinder of fine gauze is carried by the miner into an atmosphere largely charged with the explosive gas ('fire-damp,' they call it), the gas is of course kindled inside the lamp; and this is the signal for the miner to retire, since it warns him of danger. For though the flame within cannot penetrate through a perfect gauze, yet the presence of defects in the sheath (from rust or other causes) may possibly cause it to be burnt through, if exposed long to a high temperature. The safety-lamp, therefore, though not an absolute protection for any length of time, still well deserves its name; since it performs the double function of admonishing the miner as to the presence of his enemy, and of shutting in the flame from it long enough to allow him to retire to other and less dangerous parts of the workings.

89. It was stated (Art. 83) that liquids and aëriform fluids are specially bad conductors of heat. The following is an experimental proof of this in the case of water:—

Fig. 24 represents a large test-tube nearly filled with cold water, a lump of ice having been formed at the bottom of the tube by sticking it in a freezing mixture (Art. 53). The upper portion of the water is then heated by a lamp-flame and made to *boil* for some time *without melting the ice below*. This could not be done if the water were only a tolerably good conductor. There is no convection of heat down to the ice, since the heated particles of water ascend from the region of the lamp-flame to the surface.

Fig. 24.

90. **Spheroidal State of Liquids.**—When a small quantity of liquid is thrown on a metallic plate, heated considerably above the boiling-point of the liquid, the latter does not boil, but forms a spheroidal mass, the temperature of which is *below its boiling-point*. This is accounted for by the fact that the great heat evaporates the liquid on its under surface, and thus forms a *cushion of vapour* between the liquid and the metal. The low conductive power of this vapour and the high conductive power of the metallic plate cause that only a fraction of the heat enters the liquid. In this way a large drop of water will take five or six minutes to evaporate upon a surface of polished copper or silver heated to about 200° C. If the temperature of the plate be allowed to cool to a temperature not much exceeding the

boiling-point, contact takes place; the liquid boils and rapidly disappears.

This may be further illustrated by suspending a red-hot ball of platinum in a beaker of cold water. The ball is separated from the water by an envelope of steam, and contact between the water and the ball does not occur until the latter has cooled considerably.

M. Boutigny first applied this principle so as to freeze water inside a red-hot crucible. In a crucible of platinum heated to redness he placed some liquid sulphurous acid, which immediately assumed the spheroidal state, and a small portion of *water* dropped into the midst was *frozen*. Faraday went further, and by using ether and solid carbonic acid (see Art. 68) procured so low a temperature as to freeze not only water but *mercury* within the red-hot crucible.

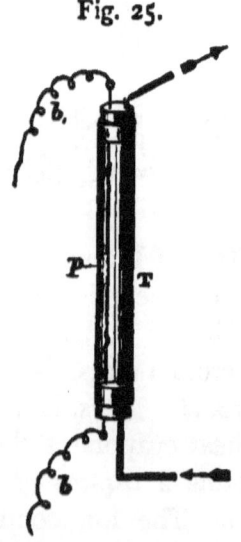

Fig. 25.

91. Although gaseous bodies generally have extremely low conductivities, **hydrogen** forms an exception to the rule; so much so that this affords—along with other data—reason for considering hydrogen (the lightest of known

bodies) to be the *vapour of a metal very much above its boiling-point*. This may be shown by a simple experiment, represented in Fig. 25.

A glass tube T is fitted with a good cork at each end, through which the wires $b\ b_1$ from an electric battery are inserted. The circuit is completed by the platinum wire p, which runs through the tube from one copper wire to the other. When an electric current is passed through the wires, the platinum wire p (owing to electrical resistance, Art. 12) becomes incandescent. This occurs when the interior of the tube T is a vacuum, and when it is filled with most ordinary gases, including those which constitute air. But when dry hydrogen is passed into T, the incandescence ceases, the heat generated by the resistance of the wire p being conducted away by the hydrogen.[1]

92. We must not omit to notice the effect of conduction upon the internal heat of the earth (Art. 11). The conductivities of some of the commoner constituents of the earth's crust (e.g. sand, sandstone, and trap-rock) have been shown to be very low as compared with those of the metals, and the earth's crust has therefore, upon the whole, a conservative influence upon its internal heat, though there is a slow, steady, flow of heat from the interior to the exterior. In the contraction which results from this continuous cooling of the globe by conduction and radiation (the amount of heat lost annually being calculated, from experiments at Edinburgh and Paris, to be sufficient to melt 777 cubic miles of ice at 0°C.), we may see a powerful cause of disturbance and dislocation of the crust of the earth; and almost all, if not all, of the phenomena connected with earthquakes and volcanic action may be, directly or indirectly, referred to this cause.[2]

[1] It will be found safer in practice to admit the hydrogen at the top in this experiment: the air is thus more completely removed.

[2] Mallett, *On Vulcanicity*.

CHAPTER V.

SPECIFIC HEAT.

93. ALL substances do *not* require the *same quantity* of *heat* to produce in them the *same elevation of temperature.* If 1 pound of water and 1 pound of mercury, both at the same temperature, be exposed for the same length of time to the same heat, the mercury will be found at the end of that time to have risen in temperature 30 times as much as the water; therefore when 1 pound of water is heated from 0° C. to 1° C., 30 times as much heat passes into the water as is required to pass into 1 pound of mercury to raise it from 0° C. to 1° C. So with other forms of matter, *different quantities of heat must pass into equal weights of them to cause the same elevation of temperature.*

The amount of heat taken up by a given weight of a body, when its temperature rises any given number of degrees, is precisely the same as that which the body gives off when its temperature sinks through the same degrees. For example, 1 pound of water heated from 0° to 30° C. absorbs 30 thermal units (units of heat, Art. 52); while the quantity of heat taken up by 1 pound of mercury, when it undergoes the same alteration of temperature, is only 1 thermal unit. When therefore 1 pound of water is cooled down from 30° to 0° C., it gives off 30 thermal units, while the pound of mercury gives off but one thermal unit; consequently a pound of mercury cooling from 30° to 0° C. (or 30

Distinction between Quantity & Temperature. 75

pounds cooling from 1° to 0° C.) would only give off enough heat to cause an elevation of 1° C. in the temperature of 1 pound of water. Water, having such a high capacity for heat, is a convenient standard by which to measure the specific heat of other bodies; and the thermal unit, as before defined (Art. 52), coincides with the **specific unit**.

The following table gives the specific heat of a number of common substances at constant pressure:—

Water . . . 1·000.

Solids.

Antimony	·051	Brass		·094
Silver	·056	Nickel		·109
Arsenic	·081	Gold		·032
Bismuth	·031	Phosphorus		·189
Cadmium	·057	Platinum		·032
Charcoal	·242	Lead		·031
Copper	·092	Plumbago		·202
Diamond	·147	Sulphur		·203
Tin	·056	Glass		·198
Iron	·114	Zinc		·096
Iodine	·054	Ice		·504

Liquids.

Mercury	·033	Benzine	·396
Acetic acid	·659	Ether	·516
Alcohol (at 36° C.)	·674	Oil of turpentine	·463

Gases and Vapours.

Oxygen	·218	Ammonia	·508
Nitrogen	·244	Steam	·481
Hydrogen	3·409	Ether	·481
Carbon dioxide	·217	Alcohol	·453

It will be observed that for liquids (except mercury, whose low specific heat adapts it admirably for thermometric use) the specific heat is far greater than that of most solids; while among the solids given in the table, carbon in two of its allotropic forms (charcoal and plumbago) and sulphur have very high capacity for heat (specific heat). Diamond, another allotropic form of carbon, has a lower specific heat than phosphorus. Water shows a striking variation in its specific heat, in the three different physical states (ice, water, and steam); thus—

	Solid.	Liquid.	Vapour.
Specific heat	·504	1	·481

94. There are two conditions under which we may consider the specific heat of gaseous bodies:—

    (1) We may consider the amount of heat required to raise a given weight 1° C. at *constant volume*.

Or (2) we may consider the amount of heat required to raise a given weight 1° C. at *constant pressure*.

Fig. 26.

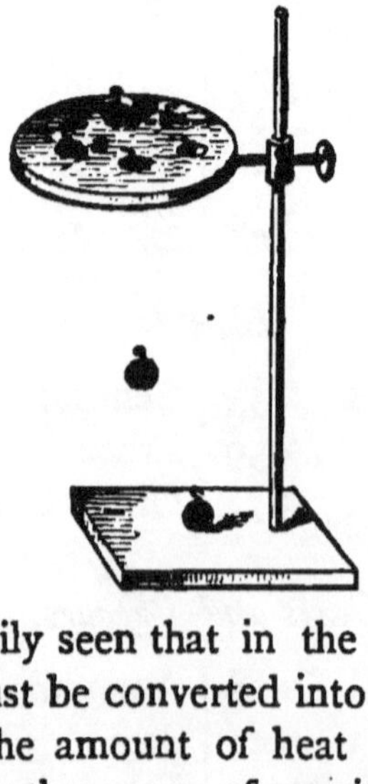

It will be readily seen that in the latter case a certain portion of heat must be converted into the work of expanding the gas; and the amount of heat thus converted into work will represent the *excess* of specific heat obtained by the latter over that obtained by the former process.

Calorimetry by Mixture, Fusion, Cooling. 77

95. We may illustrate the difference in the specific heat of different metals by a simple experiment. Five balls about two-thirds of an inch in diameter, consisting respectively of the metals iron, copper, tin, lead, bismuth, are heated by immersion in oil at a temperature of nearly 200° C. (see Fig. 26). If then they are placed upon a cake of white wax, the iron ball, having the *greatest quantity* of heat, will melt the wax fastest, the other four balls melting quantities proportionate to their specific heats. The iron ball would melt its way through, and be probably followed by the copper: the other three would remain partially embedded in the wax, more or less deeply, according to the *several quantities* of heat given off by them in cooling; i.e. according to their specific heats.

96. **Calorimetry** is the name given to the processes by which the specific heat of bodies is ascertained. They are:—

(1) The method of mixture.
(2) The method of the melting of ice.
(3) The method of cooling.
(4) By *Bunsen's Calorimeter*. (See Note IV. p. 100.)

(1) **Mixture.**—Here a known weight of a certain substance, at a known temperature, is mixed with a known weight of water at a lower temperature (say, at 0° C.). This is done rapidly, and then the temperature of the mixture is ascertained by the thermometer. If we assume that the whole quantity of heat lost by the heated substance is gained by the water, and if the *weight of the substance under investigation and of the water be the same*, we have

$$\frac{\text{No. of degrees gained by the water}}{\text{No. of degrees lost by the substance}} = \begin{cases} \text{specific heat} \\ \text{of substance.} \end{cases}$$

This method is, however, unsatisfactory, as some of the heat is lost in warming the vessel and the thermometer, while some escapes into the air.

(2) **Fusion of Ice.**—If a warm body be surrounded by ice, the heat of the body is imparted to the ice, melting some portion of it, until the temperature of the body is reduced to 0° C. The weight of melted ice being found, and the latent heat of water being 79 thermal units, it is evident that the heat given up by the substance in cooling is equal to that which has become latent in the melted ice :—

$$\therefore \frac{79 \times \text{Wt. of melted ice}}{\text{Wt. of substance} \times \text{No. of degrees lost}} = \begin{cases} \text{specific heat} \\ \text{of substance.} \end{cases}$$

The ice-vessel must be surrounded by a jacket, containing also ice, to save it from the influence of the surrounding

Fig. 27.

air. The chief objection to this method is that some of the water remains adhering to the ice, so that the *exact weight* of ice melted is not found.

The arrangement is shown in the accompanying diagram (Fig. 27). The spaces A and B are filled with broken ice; the water from A produced by the melting of the ice passes off through the tube c, is collected, and weighed.

Variation with Temperature. 79

(3) **Method by cooling.**—Here two similar substances (e.g. water and mercury) of the same temperature are exposed to the same cooling influence for the same time. It is easy to see that the one which has the smallest quantity of heat stored up in it—in other words, the one with the smallest specific heat—will cool fastest. If *equal weights* of the substances be used the fall of temperature will be in *inverse ratio* to their specific heats.

$$\therefore \frac{\text{No. of deg. lost by water}}{\text{No. of deg. lost by mercury, \&c.}} = \left\{ \begin{array}{l} \text{specific heat of} \\ \text{mercury, \&c.} \end{array} \right.$$

The specific heat of the same body generally increases with the temperature, especially near the boiling or melting point. Platinum has a remarkable constancy of specific heat through a great range of temperature, its specific heat at 1200° C. being almost the same as at 100° C. On this account it is of great use as a *Pyrometer* for measuring the heat of furnaces. A piece of platinum is held in a furnace till it has acquired the same temperature as the furnace, and then plunged into ice-cold water. From the rise of temperature in the water the heat of the furnace may be approximately calculated, the specific heat of platinum being known.

An elaborate series of experiments by Regnault showed that the specific heat of a gas at a temperature greatly above its boiling-point (Art. 62) does not increase with the rise of temperature, at least between $-30°$ and $200°$ C.; but in readily liquefiable gases this change occurs. The specific heat of carbonic anhydride, for example, is—

at $0°$ C. $= \cdot 187$
$100°$ C. $= \cdot 215$
$200°$ C. $= \cdot 240$

97. *Definition.*—The **atomic weight** of an elementary body is the weight of its atom as compared with the weight of an atom of hydrogen (see Art. 2).

As far as the ordinary elementary gases are concerned,

their specific heat is found to vary *inversely* as their atomic weights.[1] This will be seen from the following:—

Gas.	At. Wt.	Sp. Heat.	
Hydrogen	1 ×	3·409 =	3·409
Oxygen	16 ×	·218 =	3·448
Nitrogen	14 ×	·244 =	3·416

the slight difference of the numbers in the fourth column being referrible to errors of experiment.

98. The very high specific heat of water is of great practical importance. It is turned to account in such devices as railway foot-warmers, its great capacity for heat enabling it to maintain a higher temperature than the air for some hours. For the same reason the conservative influence of the ocean is very great, modifying the extremes of temperature in maritime countries. In summer it absorbs a great portion of the solar heat, without any great alteration of its own temperature, while much of the heat becomes latent in the great quantity of vapour formed. In winter a large portion of the heat of the ocean is given up to the land.

99. *Definitions:*—

(1) **Capacity** of a body for heat is the number of units of heat required to raise unit of mass of that body one degree of temperature.

(2) 'The **specific-heat** of a body is the ratio of the quantity of heat required to raise that body one degree to the quantity required to raise an equal weight of water one degree' (Clerk-Maxwell).

It is found that the same quantity of heat produces always the same thermal effects, which are in no way altered by the nature of its source.

---

[1] Commonly referred to as 'Dulong & Petit's Law.'

CHAPTER VI.

RADIANT ENERGY.

100. When two bodies at different temperatures are placed opposite each other, an unequal exchange of heat takes place across the intervening space: the temperature of the hotter body falls; that of the colder one rises by virtue of heat

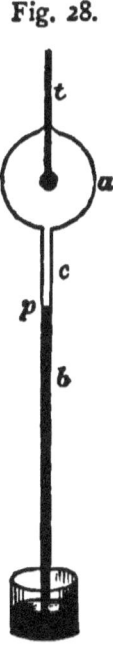

Fig. 28.

received from the hotter. In this way the earth is warmed by the sun's heat; and it is clear that the transmission of solar heat to the earth does not depend upon any ponderable intervening medium. Nor does it depend upon light, as Rumford has shown by the following experiment.

A barometer-tube *b* expanded at one end into a globe *a* is taken; and into the latter a thermometer *t* is inserted, the bulb being hermetically sealed to it. The tube and globe, being filled with mercury, are inverted, and the tube being more than 760 mm in length, the mercury sinks to the level *p*, leaving a 'Torricellian' vacuum above. The globe is then cut off from the tube by melting the tube at *c*, in the flame of the blowpipe, and drawing it out to a point. When this is done, the bulb of the thermometer is shut off from all communication with the outer air; so that if any heat passes inwards to the thermometer, it must do so by direct **radiation**, and not by conduction. When the globe is immersed in hot water, the thermometer is observed to rise much more than can be accounted for by the heating of its stem. This shows that *radiant heat does not depend upon light.*

A thermometer, the bulb of which is coated with lampblack and is entirely enclosed within a vacuum, so as to prevent conduction of heat, is generally used to measure the heating power of the sun's rays.

These and many other phenomena connected with heat and light can only be explained by assuming the existence of a subtile fluid, or *ether* (an imponderable medium), which pervades all space, but is of such extreme tenuity as to be quite imperceptible to the most refined senses, and is not affected by the heat which passes through it.

101. Heat transmitted by this medium is said to **radiate**, and is called **Radiant Heat**. We have seen that when heat is *conducted* through ponderable matter, such as a bar of metal, its passage is more or less gradual; but the *radiation* of heat is practically instantaneous, being at the rate of about 190,000 miles per second. This is a conclusion drawn from the results of a great many experiments, which go to prove that light and heat are only varieties of the same kind of energy; and the rate at which light travels has been measured by observation of the satellites of Jupiter. Radiant heat and light being both regarded as an *undulatory or wave-*

like motion in the same medium, the difference of their effects is connected with the difference in the *amplitude of their waves.* We must remember that radiant energy has none of the characteristics of heat, and that this is only developed when the passage of radiant energy is interrupted by any substance which is not perfectly 'diathermanous.'

102. **Dark and Luminous Heat.**—When a beam of sunlight is admitted through a chink into a dark room, and allowed to fall upon one of the plane surfaces of a prism of glass, represented in section in Fig. 29, the *white light* is split up into rays of seven different colours, because the rays of these several colours are **refracted,** or bent, at different angles. If therefore the beam of light, after emerging from

Fig. 29.

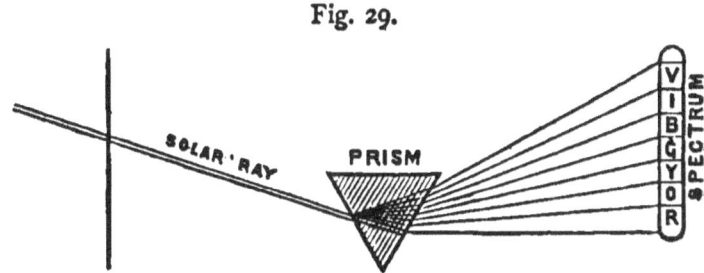

the other side of the prism, be allowed to fall upon a dark screen, a **spectrum** will be formed, showing the seven colours violet, indigo, blue, green, yellow, orange, red. This is because the *violet* rays are bent upwards most, the indigo rays next, and so on, the *red* rays being bent least of all. This was discovered by Newton, but Herschel was the first to notice that the *heat* of the spectrum is not the same at all points, but gradually *increases towards the red* ; and not only so, but that *beyond the red, where no light falls, greater heat is found than in any part of the luminous or visible spectrum.* We can thus distinguish two kinds of heat :—

(1) *Luminous heat,* in which the rays of heat are combined with light.

(2) *Dark heat,* where light is absent.

103. This will be better understood by reference to Fig. 30, where the different degrees of intensity of heat are denoted by the length of the dotted lines; the curve which connects their upper extremities may therefore be called the *curve of intensity* of the heat rays of the spectrum.

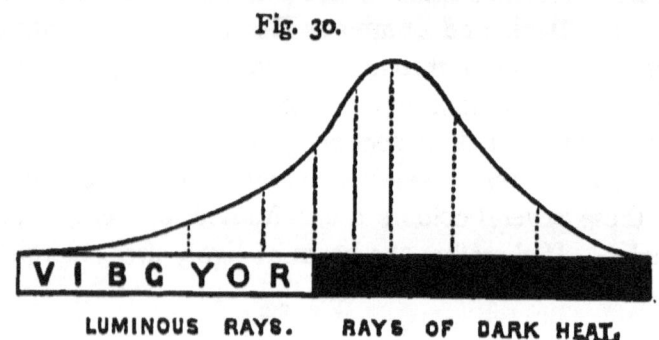

Fig. 30.

LUMINOUS RAYS.   RAYS OF DARK HEAT.

The refrangibility and colour of each ray being determined by its particular *wave-length*, we understand why a ball of metal possesses different optical properties at different temperatures. At a dark heat it gives off rays comparatively large (exceeding ·000,812 mm length), no luminous effect being produced; and these succeed one another with increasing rapidity as the temperature rises. After a time red rays (of ·00065 mm length) are emitted, along with the larger ones. And when white heat is reached, waves of still less wave-length (·0005 mm and less) are mingled with those of greater amplitude.

It is important thus to distinguish between luminous and dark heat, since some substances which allow rays of one kind to pass through them absorb rays of the other kind.

Luminous heat passes readily through glass, rock-crystal, ice, and most substances which are transparent.

Dark heat passes less readily through rock-crystal and glass, which absorb a portion of it, while a greater portion of it is stopped by alum (either crystalline or in a saturated solution), and ice entirely absorbs dark heat.

Heat-rays of the Spectrum.

This law explains why heat from the sun accumulates in greenhouses and glass frames. The *luminous* heat passes readily through the glass, and is absorbed by the ground or other opaque substances. These give it off by radiation, but as *dark* heat, which does not pass out again through the glass so readily as the luminous rays pass inwards. We can therefore literally 'bottle-up' solar heat.

Though colour has little effect upon dark heat, it often affects the absorption of luminous heat, especially in substances such as cloth, cotton, wool, and other organic substances, which are powerful absorbents. A white garment therefore *absorbs* less of the sun's heat than a coloured or black one. (Comp. Art. 106.)

104. By substituting a lens for the prism in Fig. 29, a series of parallel rays of heat may be refracted so as to converge to a single point (focus), as with the common *burning-glass*, or with a lens of clear *ice*.

105. **Radiation.**—We are all familiar with the fact that the

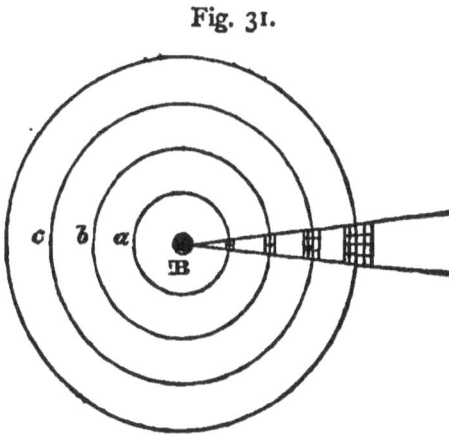

Fig. 31.

heat given out from any source is greater or less according as we are nearer to, or farther from, that source; and the same is true for light.

In Fig. 31 let B represent a red-hot ball of metal, the

circle *b* being twice the distance of the circle *a* from the ball, and circle *c* thrice that distance. An object placed in the circumference of *a* will receive *four times* as much heat as if it be placed in the circumference of *b*, and *nine times* as much as if it be placed in the circumference of *c*, and so on. This can be easily understood, if we remember that the surface of a sphere increases in the same ratio as the square of its radius. Now, the heat given out from the ball radiates equally in all directions, and we may conceive a hollow sphere whose inner surface is made up of an indefinite number of small planes, all placed at the distance of the circle *a* from the ball; and this surface would receive *the whole quantity of heat* radiated from the ball. If this heat be allowed to travel twice as far in all directions, so as to fall on the inner surface of a hollow sphere, which is represented in section by the circle *b*, and supposed to be made up of an indefinite number of planes of the *same size* as those forming the surface of *a*—since the surface of *b* contains four times as many of these planes, and *the same quantity of heat is distributed over them all*, it follows that *each plane* of the sphere *b* can only receive one-fourth the amount of heat received by each plane in the sphere *a*. In a similar way we may reason for *c*, and so on for any number of circles.

Hence the law of radiation :—

The heat received by a body varies **inversely** *as the square of the distance from the source.*

It is known as the **law of inverse squares**. Other circumstances which modify the heating effects are—

(1) The intensity of the source of heat.

(2) It can be proved by experiment that when heat is radiated from a surface it is radiated most in the direction perpendicular to that surface.

(3) When heat is imparted by a hot to a cold body the radiation goes on more rapidly the greater the difference between the temperatures of the two bodies.

Since all bodies are constantly giving off heat; when the

temperature of a body rises, it does so because the heat it receives is greater than that which it gives out; on the other hand, when the temperature of a body falls, it gives out more heat than it receives. (See Art. 5.) This is the **Theory of Exchanges.**

106. The rapidity with which heat is radiated from a body depends very much on the nature of its surface. If a cubical metal canister (commonly known as *Leslie's Cube*) have one of its surfaces coated with lampblack or white lead; a second with Indian ink; a third with mercury; and the fourth with tin, gold, silver, or copper; and the cube be filled with water at 100° C.; the radiation from the four surfaces, as shown by the thermopile, will be as follows:—

Radiation from surface of lampblack or white lead   100
,,   ,,   indian ink   88
,,   ,,   mercury . . .   20
,,   ,,   tin, gold, silver, or copper   12

It would appear from the first result that the radiation is not influenced by a black or white surface. Neither does colour affect *dark* heat, as Prof. Tyndall has shown. He found that when the surfaces of the cube were covered by velvet of different colours, the radiation was the same from all. The colour of clothes therefore has no effect upon the amount of heat *radiated* from the human body. (comp. Art. 103.)

A body with a rough surface radiates heat faster than one of the same material with a polished surface.

107. When rays of heat strike against a body—

(1) A portion is **absorbed,** and produces heat within the body.

(2) A portion is **reflected,** or thrown back from the surface.

(3) A portion is **dispersed,** or scattered irregularly.

108. **Absorption.**—When radiant heat passes into a mass,

the body is said to absorb heat. As the rays fall more directly upon the surface of a body, more of this heat is absorbed; solar heat therefore heats the ground more in summer than in winter, from the more direct incidence of the sun's rays in summer.

Those bodies which radiate heat most are the best absorbents, *the radiating and absorbent power of the same substance being always equal.* The above table of relative radiating powers of several substances will therefore show equally well their relative absorbing powers for dark heat (Art. 106).

A remarkable difference is found in the absorbing powers of gases. Air (oxygen and nitrogen) and hydrogen have equal, and extremely small, absorbing power. Chlorine absorbs 39 times, carbon dioxide 90 times, and ammonia nearly 1,200 times as much. Those gases, however, which are the best absorbers are also the best radiators.

109. Substances which allow the greater part of the heat which enters them to pass through them are said to be **diathermanous.** Such are oxygen, hydrogen, and nitrogen among gases; while among solids *rock-salt* is remarkable for this property. A ray of solar heat may therefore be easily separated from its light by a plate of rock-salt coated with lampblack or iodine. The dark coating bars the passage of the light, but allows the heat to pass on through the rock-salt plate. Diathermancy is analogous to transparency.

Dry air being a poor absorbent of heat, we can easily understand why the atmosphere is so much colder at high altitudes, as it allows the heat of the sun to pass with very slight diminution to the earth. On the other hand this very property of air accounts for what would otherwise appear the extraordinary coldness of an Indian or Australian night, which is sometimes severe enough to freeze water. Nocturnal radiation goes on so rapidly that ice is frequently formed in Bengal by simply placing shallow pans of water upon beds of straw or dry leaves, to serve as a non-conductor between the pans and the ground; while in the interior of Australia the thermometer often registers a difference of 40° C. in twenty-four hours. These results could not be obtained if moisture were present in the air in any considerable quantity, since *water-vapour is a very powerful absorbent of dark heat*. As, however, it absorbs a very small proportion of luminous heat, even when the air is nearly saturated, the heat of the sun during the day passes without much loss to the earth. From this on a *dry* night it would be radiated in the form of dark heat, but on a *damp or cloudy* night nocturnal radiation is checked, the water-vapour acting as a blanket to retain the heat in the ground.

Dew is water-vapour deposited upon terrestrial objects, which have parted by radiation with so much heat that their temperature has fallen below the dew-point of the air (Art. 65).

Hoar-frost is frozen dew, and is formed when vapour is deposited upon the ground and other objects whose temperature is below the freezing-point. (Comp. Art. 71.)

110. **Reflection.**—When radiant heat falls upon a surface, some of it is thrown back, or **reflected**. It will be seen at once that surfaces which absorb most heat reflect the least, and vice versâ. A polished surface is a good reflector but a bad absorbent; consequently a dull fender is often very hot while the polished fire-irons are comparatively cool. If a hot metal ball be placed equally distant between two disks of metal, one of which has, facing the ball, a polished surface, and the other a surface coated with lampblack, and a piece of phosphorus be placed behind each disk, the greater absorbent power of the dull surface will be shown by the phosphorus behind it taking fire sooner than that behind the other. So also those surfaces which reflect most heat are the poorest radiators; a polished metal tea-pot therefore retains heat better than an earthenware one. We may express the law thus :—

The radiating and absorbing powers of a surface being equal, each is in **inverse** *ratio to the reflecting power of that surface.*

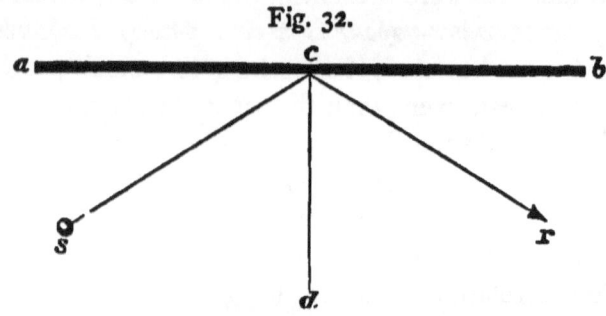

Fig. 32.

In Fig. 32 let *a b* represent a plane surface, near which is placed a hot ball of metal *s*. Now, since heat is given out from this source in all directions, some of this will fall upon the surface *a b*. Let us confine our attention to the ray which strikes the surface at the point *c*. A portion of this will enter the substance of the material, but if the plate *a b* be of highly polished metal, nearly the whole of the *incident* ray will be *reflected* in the direction of the line *c r*. If now the straight line *c d* be drawn perpendicular to *a b* (and called the *normal*), the angle *s c d* will be the angle of incidence, and the angle *r c d* the angle of reflection. And these two angles are always equal to one another; hence the **laws of reflection** :—

(1) *The angle of incidence is equal to the angle of reflection.*

(2) *The incident ray, reflected ray, and normal are in the same plane.*

111. Suppose a number of rays of heat moving in a straight line and parallel to one another strike upon a concave polished surface (such as is represented by *m n* in Fig. 33), which is an arc of a sphere with its centre at *c*; then since the angle of incidence of each ray is equal to its

angle of reflection, the rays $a\,b$, $d\,e$, $f\,g$, $h\,i$, $k\,l$, $q\,r$, $s\,t$, ... will all, after striking against the concave reflector, be brought to one point, or *focus*, at f, which

Fig. 33.

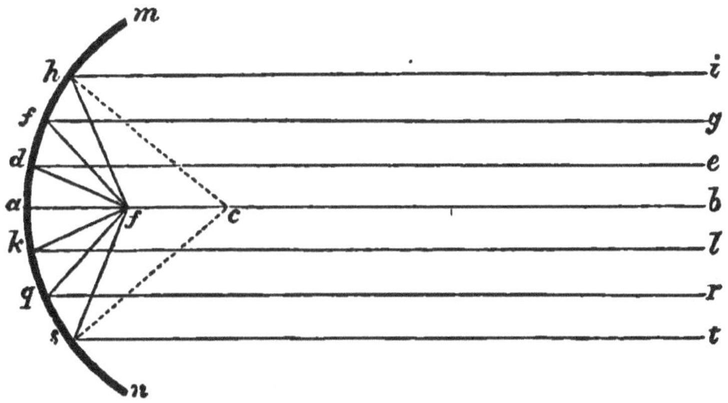

for the arc of a sphere is half-way between the centre and the surface.

This may be proved experimentally by using two concave reflectors (conjugate reflectors), which are placed some distance apart, so as to face one another. If a red-hot ball be placed in the focus of one, the heat is thrown by its reflector in parallel lines upon the other, and a thermometer-bulb, placed in the focus of the second, shows a rise of several degrees, though it is not so affected unless placed in the focus. The same thing happens if the positions of the source of heat and the thermometer are reversed. If a piece of phosphorus is substituted for the thermometer-bulb, it is ignited. Foci thus related to one another are said to be *conjugate*.

The laws of Reflection are the same for both Heat and Light. That these are but different properties of rays of the same nature is further shown by their action upon the *Radiometer*. (See Note V. p. 101.)

CHAPTER VII.

HEAT AND WORK.

112. Energy can only be estimated by its power to produce **motion**—in other words, by the **work** which it does. Now, in order that heat may perform work of any special nature it must be directed by suitable machines. And this is all a machine can do : *it can direct and utilise energy, but it cannot create it.* Let us consider a few examples of
Conversion of heat into work.

(1) The heat produced by the combustion of fuel in the furnace of a steam-engine is imparted to the water in the boiler, and by the expansive force it gives to the steam, moves the piston, with which are connected all the parts of the machinery to be set in motion.

(2) The heat of the sun lifts up, in the form of vapour, the water of seas, lakes, &c., and this being deposited upon higher regions, forms, under the influence of gravity, a descending current of water, which can be made to turn a water-wheel connected with machinery.

(3) Solar energy is expended in the vital processes that go on in plants, whereby are formed, from the raw materials of the ground and air, all our **food** and **fuel**. A ton of hay eaten by a horse, and after digestion going to make good the waste within, would by *muscular energy* do far more work than if the same quantity were used as fuel in a furnace. If therefore food and fuel cost the same, the horse would be a far more economical machine than the engine. We must

not, however, forget that the horse requires food at all times, the engine fuel only when at work. The great advantage of the steam-engine arises from the concentration of energy.

The heat obtained by the consumption of nearly 100,000,000 tons of coal yearly in the British Islands is so much energy of the sun's rays, stored up in long-by-gone ages, in the vegetation which formed the chief material of coal. This is set free in the process of combustion (the main part of which consists in the combination of the coal's carbon and hydrogen with the air's oxygen), and is given back in the form of heat.

Conversion of work into heat has been already illustrated. (Ch. I.)

113. It is a law of Thermodynamics that *when equal quantities of mechanical effect are produced from purely thermal sources, or are lost in producing thermal effects, then equal quantities of heat are put out of existence or generated.*

Of late years many physicists, and especially Dr. Joule'[1] of Manchester, have investigated the connection between heat and work. By a number of laborious experiments—such as (1) ascertaining the amount of heat produced by compression of air in a vessel under water, the mechanical energy applied for this purpose being known ; (2) the friction of a brass paddle-wheel in mercury, when made to rotate by cards attached to falling weights—Joule found that the quantity of heat required to raise the temperature of one pound of water 1° F. would, if applied to air confined in a cylinder furnished with a piston, raise 772 pounds through one foot ; and conversely the mechanical force required to raise 772 pounds through one foot (or one pound through 772 feet) would, if expended in producing heat, furnish enough to raise the temperature of one pound of water 1° F.

[1] Count Rumford, Colding, Davy, and especially Helmholtz, have also contributed greatly to the establishment of the theory of Thermodynamics.

∴ 772 foot-pounds=Mechanical Equivalent of heat.

(If the Cent. scale is used in these calculations, the mech. equiv. of course $= 772 \times \frac{9}{5} =$ nearly 1390 foot-pounds.)

114. Conservation and Dissipation of Energy.—Wherever energy is displayed, its tendency is to overcome resistance to motion. This is **kinetic** energy (Gr. κινέω, to set in motion). By 'conservation of energy' we mean that *the sum-total of the energy of the universe is always the same*, notwithstanding the transmutation of any one force into others.

We have had to notice instances in which energy ceases for a time to be active.

(1) The solar energy which has been used in the development of the vegetal materials of the coal-seams lies dormant, and has done so for countless ages, embedded in the earth. Though not in actual operation, it must still be considered as latent in the coal, since the whole of it is restored in the kinetic form, when the carbon and hydrogen of the coal are raised to a sufficient temperature, in contact with oxygen, to set agoing a rapid process of combination between them and the oxygen (combustion). And this kinetic energy can be controlled and made effective for special ends by suitable machinery.

(2) When solar energy is expended in evaporating water, it is not lost: some of it is given back as heat to the atmosphere, when the vapour condenses to the liquid state; the remainder becomes kinetic by the descent of the head of water under the influence of gravitation

(3) When a stone is thrown or carried up to an eminence, kinetic energy is expended, but it is not lost; since the stone is placed thereby in a **position of advantage** under the influence of gravity, as soon as all obstacles to its descent are removed. Similarly when a clock is wound up.

In all such cases, where kinetic energy is used in placing things in a position or a condition of advantage for reproducing

Dissipation of Energy. 95

kinetic energy, the energy is said to be transformed from kinetic into **potential energy.**

115. Yet in the most perfect machine some loss of energy available for work is inevitable, since no machinery can work without some slight amount of friction; and this friction, however slight, developes heat, which radiates into space. Such a thing as 'perpetual motion' is therefore simply impossible in machinery. Again, even in the best constructed steam-engines, the amount of energy made available for work is always considerably less than that which warms the engine, and then escapes by radiation from its surface, added to the heat which is lost by condensation of the steam when it escapes into the air, as it does in all high-pressure steam-engines. So also with human or horse labour. We may employ a number of labourers or a number of horses to pump up water, and utilise the kinetic energy of this water in its descent; but the total energy of the descending head of water is in all cases *less* than that which was expended in raising it to an eminence. Some of the animal energy expended in pumping up the water is necessarily converted into animal heat, and passes off into space by radiation, while a small portion also is, by the friction of the pumps in the first instance, and of the water-wheel subsequently, converted into heat, and radiates away. In all cases, therefore, where it is possible for energy to be converted into heat, there is a *leakage from the general stock of available energy.* This is known as the **dissipation** of energy. And as in the operation of artificial machines this dissipation is constantly going on, so also does it go on, on a much larger scale, in the operations of nature; so that we can conceive of no means by which even the heat of the sun is maintained, which shall not be, at some distant time, exhausted, leaving the centre of our system to roll as a dark black orb through space. And so with those other suns (the stars), which are probably the centres of heat and light and life to other systems.

This result follows inevitably from the known and

demonstrable doctrine of dissipation of energy, unless some provision (to which the present state of things affords no clue) exists for its recuperation. If this be not admitted as probable, we pass to the other 'horn of the dilemma.' For if dissipation is not followed by recuperation, we are as much at a loss to explain how matter in the universe came at first to be placed in a condition of advantage ; and it seems impossible to conceive (on any scientific grounds) how—even on the *nebular hypothesis*—matter existed once in an extremely attenuated state, without as much energy being put into it as it is capable of giving off as heat by condensation and chemical action. This is as inexplicable as any conjectural process of recuperation. To account for the one or the other we must assume the existence of a Cause which is præter-scientific.

NOTE I.

On the Tension of Water-vapour.

(1.) In Art. 73, ebullition was shown to occur when the tension of the steam is sufficient to enable it to overcome the atmospheric pressure. It is clear that for any temperature below that required for ebullition we shall always get the following equation :

$$P = B + T.$$

Where P = atmospheric pressure, B = the weight of the column of mercury in the long arm of the tube (Fig. 19), and T = the tension of the water-vapour for any given temperature. Now, with P constant, as the value of T increases with every rise of temperature, the height of the barometric column (and consequently the value of B) must be lessened ; and, of course, when the boiling-point is reached, B vanishes, and we get for the above equation :

$$P = T.$$

And this is equivalent to the third law of ebullition.

(2.) We have also seen (Art. 74) that the temperature of steam (and accordingly its tension) may be increased by confining it within a vessel of sufficient strength. When the digester is furnished with a loaded safety-valve, the tension of the steam goes on rising until it is able to lift the loaded valve and escape ; if (e.g.) the valve be loaded with $29\frac{1}{2}$ lbs., the water will continue to boil at 120° C., the temperature being shown by a thermometer which is inserted through the top of the digester. In this way the tension in lbs. of steam at the temperatures between 100° C. and 230° C. were ascertained by Regnault. The weight of the load on the valve may be in each case expressed in millimetres of a mercurial column.

From these two methods the following results have been obtained ; and in a similar manner the tension of other vapours may be ascertained.

H

Tension of Aqueous Vapour in millimetres of mercury (*Regnault*).
Temperatures expressed in Cent. degrees.

Temperature.	Tension in Millimetres (Elastic force).	Temperature.	Tension in Millimetres (Elastic force).
deg.	mm.	·deg.	mm.
−32	0·320	65	186·945
−30	0·386	70	233·093
−25	0·605	75	288·517
−20	0·927	80	354·643
−15	1·400	85	433·041
−10	2·093	90	525·450
−5	3·113	95	633·778
0	4·600	100	760·000
+5	6·534	110	1075·37
10	9·165	120	1491·28
15	12·699	130	2030·28
20	17·391	140	2717·63
25	23·550	150	3581·23
30	31·548	160	4651·62
35	41·827	170	5961·66
40	54·906	180	7546·39
45	71·391	190	9442·70
50	91·982	200	11688·96
55	117·478	210	14324·80
60	148·791	220	17390·36
		230	20926·40

NOTE II.
On the Metric System.

It is most useful for all scientific calculations, on account of its decimal principle of reduction.

Its unit of length is the *metre* (= 39·37 inches).

Fractions of this are expressed by using Latin numerals as prefixes; thus, *deci- centi- milli-* metre.

Multiples of it are expressed by using Greek numerals as prefixes, thus, *deka- hecto- kilo-* metre.

Measures of capacity are determined by taking the cubes of the metre, and of its fractions and multiples.

1 *litre* $\begin{cases} = 1,000 \text{ cubic centimetres ('ccm.').} \\ = 1 \text{ cubic decimetre ('cdm.').} \\ = \frac{1}{1000} \text{ cubic metre ('cub. m.').} \end{cases}$

1 *gramme* $\begin{cases} = \text{unit of weight.} \\ = \text{wt. of 1 ccm. of distilled water at 4° C.} \\ = 15\cdot432 \text{ grains.} \end{cases}$

NOTE III.
On the Kinetic Theory of Heat.

THE theory [that heat is the result of molecular motions, or vibrations] was powerfully advocated by Count Rumford, and by Davy, who, in the early part of the present century, instituted an important series of experiments upon the production of heat by friction. Many philosophers were subsequently induced to adopt the theory of the vibratory nature of heat as maintained by these eminent men. The opinions of Davy upon this subject are thus stated by him in his treatise on 'Chemical Philosophy,' p. 95: 'It seems possible to account for all the phenomena of heat, if it be supposed that in solids the particles are in a constant state of vibratory motion, the particles of the hottest bodies moving with the greatest velocity and through the greatest space; that in fluids and elastic fluids, besides the vibratory motion, which must be conceived greatest in the last, the particles have a motion round their own axes, with different velocities, the particles of elastic fluids moving with the greatest quickness; and that in ethereal substances the particles move round their own axes, and separate from each other, penetrating in straight lines through space. Temperature may be conceived to be dependent upon the velocities of the vibrations; increase of capacity on the motion being performed in greater space; and the diminution of temperature, during the conversion of solids into fluids or gases, may be explained on the idea of the loss of vibratory motion, in consequence of the revolution of the particles round their axes, at the moment when the body becomes fluid or aëriform, or from the loss of rapidity of vibration in consequence of the motion of the particles through greater space.'
—Prof. Miller, 'Chemical Physics,' p. 262.

NOTE IV.
Bunsen's Calorimeter.

The principle made use of in the construction of this instrument is the change of volume which water undergoes when it passes from the liquid to the solid state, and *vice versâ*. The calorimeter (c) (fig. 34) is filled with pure de-aërated water (Art. 78) at 0° C. except a space (M) at the bottom which is occupied by mercury; the mercury also fills the tube which communicates with the interior of the calorimeter at one end, and at the other end opens into the air. The instrument thus constructed is embedded in pure fresh-fallen snow (s). This soon acquires, and retains for a considerable time, the temperature of 0° C. if placed in a room not below the freezing temperature.

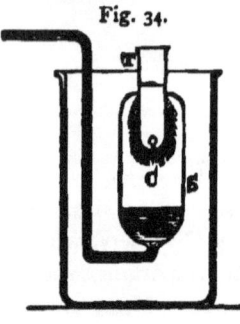
Fig. 34.

To prepare the instrument for use, the test-tube (T), which is to receive the body whose specific heat is to be investigated, has a stream of some volatile liquid, such as ether or alcohol, previously cooled by a frigorific mixture (Art. 53), driven through it. As a result of this, a portion of the water in c is converted into ice in contact with the exterior of the test-tube (Arts. 63, 70). The expansion of the water as it freezes drives a portion of the mercury through the tube; and this being graduated on the horizontal arm, the position of the mercury, when the instrument is ready for use, is easily noted.

The lump of metal (or other solid) to be examined is raised to a known temperature (say 100° C.) by being held for some time in a current of steam; it is then dropped as quickly as possible into the water which is placed in the tube T, and cooled down to the temperature (0° C.) of the encrusting ice. The heat of the small solid is imparted to the cold water in the test-tube T; but owing to the great capacity for heat which the water possesses (Art. 93), its temperature is only slightly raised, and, not being heated above 4° C., it is condensed, and remains in the bottom of the tube. The upper portion of the water in T being a bad conductor, the exchange of heat takes place between the water at the bottom of T and the ice in c, by conduction through the walls of the tube; and the quantity of ice melted thereby will of course vary with the amount of heat given off by different bodies during cooling. The contraction which accompanies liquefaction allows the atmospheric pressure to drive the mercury inwards, and a comparison of the distances traversed by the end of the thread of mercury in different instances enables the experimenter to compare accurately the thermal capacities of the bodies examined.

NOTE V.
Crookes' Radiometer.

This interesting instrument, as now usually constructed, consists of several (usually 4) discs of burnt mica attached to exceedingly fine wires, which are supported by a small sharply-pointed needle turning freely in a cup-shaped hollow at the summit of a pillar of glass, which is hermetically sealed within a bulb and tube (see fig. 35). From this last the air has been withdrawn by means of a Sprengel air-pump, so as to produce as complete a vacuum as possible. The discs of mica are blackened on one side to render them highly absorbent (Art. 108), and retain their highly-reflecting surfaces on the other, but so that all the surfaces of each kind shall face in the same direction of rotation. When radiant energy, either 'dark' or 'luminous' (Art. 102), falls upon the bulb, and, passing across the vacuous space, impinges upon the surfaces of the discs, the blackened surfaces are repelled with a rapidity proportioned to the strength of the radiation and the difference between the absorbing powers of the two kinds of surfaces.

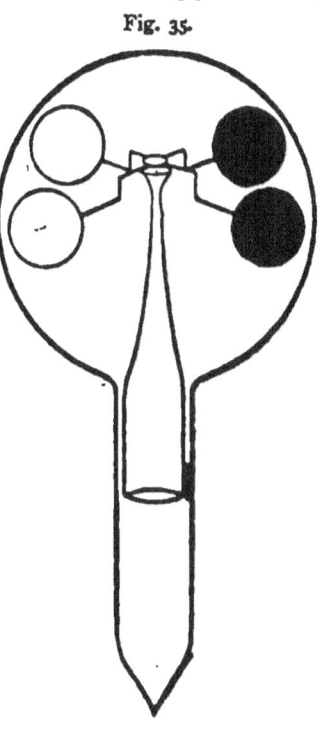

Fig. 35.

The rapidity of rotation, and therefore the strength of the radiation falling upon the instrument, is found, on exposing it to the various dispersed rays of the spectrum (Art. 103), to vary in a manner which corresponds with the results given by a delicate thermometer or by the thermo-pile. The results obtained in this way by the inventor of the instrument are thus stated:

Ultra red 100	Green	41
Extreme red . . 85	Blue	22
Red 73	Indigo . . .	8·5
Orange 66	Violet . . .	6
Yellow 41	Ultra violet . .	5

GLOSSARY.

ABSORPTION (Lat. *ab*, from ; *sorbeo*, I suck in). The reception and retention within themselves, by certain bodies, of the radiant heat that falls upon their surfaces. *Absorbent*, capable of absorption.

ACCELERATE (Lat. *ad*, to ; *celero*, I hasten). To hasten a process ; to increase the velocity of a body in motion.

ADHESION (Lat. *ad + hæreo*, I stick). A property by which one body holds to another.

ADIABATIC (Gr. ἀ, not ; διά, through ; βαίνω, I go). Impermeable to heat.

AËRIFORM (Lat. *aër*, air ; *forma*, form). Applied to bodies that have the same general properties as air ; gases and vapours.

AFFINITY (Lat. *ad + finis*, end or limit). Natural attraction or relationship. 'Chemical affinity,' tendency to combine.

ALLOTROPIC (Gr. ἄλλος, other ; τρόπος, turning, fashion). Applied to the different physical conditions assumed by bodies that are chemically the same.

ALLOY (Fr. *à la loi*, according to the law). A baser metal mixed with gold, as in coinage ; any mixture of metals (mercury excepted) when in the molten state. A combination of *mercury* and any other metal is called an *amalgam*.

ANHYDRIDE (Gr. ἀ, not ; ὕδωρ, water). A compound containing oxygen, but not hydrogen ; an anhydrous acid oxide.

ASBESTOS (Gr. ἀ + σβέννυμι, I extinguish). A fibrous silicate of magnesia, of the hornblende group ; so named from its power to resist the action of fire.

ATMOSPHERE (Gr. ἀτμός, smoke or vapour ; σφαῖρα, a globe). The aëriform mass which envelopes the earth to a height of 50 miles or more.

ATOM (Gr. ἀ + τέμνω, I cut). Minute particles of matter which (theoretically considered) are absolutely indivisible.

BAROMETER (Gr. βάρος, weight ; μέτρον, measure). An instrument for showing the pressure of the atmosphere.

CALIBRATE. To measure the calibre of a tube, &c.

Glossary. 103

CALIBRE, CALIBER (Fr. *calibre*, the bore of a gun; Lat. *quâ librâ*, of what weight). The diameter of a bullet, of a column, of a tube.

CALORIMETRY (Lat. *calor*, heat; Gr. μέτρον). The measurement of *quantities* of heat.

CAPILLARY (Lat. *capillus*, hair). Applied to tubes with very fine bore, and to the motion of liquids in such tubes.

CARBONACEOUS (Lat. *carbo*, charcoal). Partly composed of carbon. Most organic bodies are so.

CARBONATE. A substance formed by the combination of carbonic anhydride with water or a metallic oxide.

CENTIGRADE (Lat. *centum*, 100; *gradus*, step). Applied to the thermometric scale (*see* Art. 19).

CHEMISTRY (Arab. *al-chemia*, the 'Black, or Egyptian Art,' from *Chemia*, the ancient name of Egypt; alchemy). The science which treats of the composition of bodies. Modern chemistry may be said to date its rise from the discovery of oxygen, by Priestley in 1774, and by Scheele in 1775.

COEFFICIENT (Lat. *con + efficiens*, from *facio*, I make). In a mathematical or scientific sense, a factor or number which shows how many times a quantity is to be taken.

COHESION (Lat. *con + hæreo*). The force which holds together the particles of a solid body.

COMBINATION (Lat. *con + bini*, two at a time). In chemistry the union of elementary bodies to form compounds.

COMBUSTION (Lat. *comburo*, I burn up). The action of fire. 'Combustible,' easily acted on by fire.

CONGELATION (Lat. *con + gelu*, ice, frost). The freezing process.

CONJUGATE (Lat. *con + jugo*, I yoke).

CONNOTE (Lat. *con + noto*, I distinguish by a mark). By a 'connotative term' logicians understand one that indicates a subject and implies an attribute.

CONSERVATION (Lat. *con + servo*, I preserve). 'Conservation of energy,' the preservation of energy in a form available for work.

CONVECTION (Lat. *con + veho*, I carry). Motion in the particles of a fluid resulting from inequality of density of different parts. In this way heat is *carried* through fluids.

CRYOPHORUS (Gr. κρύος, frost; φορός, bearing). So called from its mode of action in freezing water by the application of a freezing mixture at a distance.

CUBICAL (Gr. κύβος, a die). Of three dimensions—length, breadth, and thickness.

DECREMENT (Lat. *decrementum*, diminution). Decrease by a definite quantity.

DEFLECT (Lat. *de*, from ; *flecto*, I bend). To bend or turn aside from the normal direction.

DEMONSTRATION (Lat. *de + monstro*, I show). Certain proof.

DIATHERMANOUS (Gr. διά, through ; θερμός, heat). Permeable to radiant heat. A body which becomes heated by the passage of heat-rays into it, is said to be ATHERMANOUS.

DIFFUSION (Lat. *dis*, apart ; *fundo*, I pour). A property characteristic of gases. The *times* of their diffusion are as the *square roots* of their densities.

DISSIPATION (Lat. *dissipo*, I scatter). 'Dissipation of energy,' the conversion of energy into such a form that it cannot again be made available for producing motion.

EBULLITION (Lat. *ebullio*, I boil up). The state of boiling.

ELASTICITY (Fr. *élastique*; Gr. ἐλαύνω, I drive). Springiness; power to recover original volume. *Syn.* 'tension.'

ELECTRICITY (Gr. ἤλεκτρον, amber, in which the property was first discovered). Two opposite phases of energy ('positive' and 'negative') developed in bodies, by virtue of which they become capable of mutual attraction and repulsion.

ELEMENTS (Lat. *elementa*, first principles). In modern chemistry, those simple bodies out of which the chemist has never been able to procure more than one kind of matter.

ENERGY (Gr. ἐνέργεια = ἐν, in + ἔργον, work). The power of doing work ; in physics, of producing motion.

EQUILIBRIUM (Lat. *aquus*, equal ; *libra*, a balance). Equality of weight or force.

EQUIVALENT (Lat. *aquus + valeo*, I am strong). That which is equal to another in strength, power, or force.

EXPERIMENT (Lat. *experimentum*, a trial). The arrangement of a given set of causes in order to estimate the results that follow from their combined action. 'Experimental law,' a law or general sequence in nature admitting of demonstration by experiment.

FOCUS (Lat., a fireplace). A point to which a number of rays converge after reflection or refraction.

FORMULA (Lat. dim. of *forma*). A general expression.

FRICTION (Lat. *frico*, I rub). *See* Art. 6.

GALVANOMETER (It. *Galvani* + Gr. μέτρον). An instrument for indicating the strength and direction of a galvanic current. *Galvanism*, production of electricity by chemical action; named from its discoverer, a native of Bologna, who died in 1798.

GLOBULE (dim. of Lat. *globus*, a ball). A small drop of a liquid.

GRADUATE (Lat. *gradus*). To mark with degrees.

Glossary.

GRAVITY, GRAVITATION (Lat. *gravis*, heavy). That force by which all bodies are attracted to one another proportionally to their mass, and inversely to the square of their distance apart.

HERMETICAL (Gr. 'Ερμῆs, fabled inventor of chemistry). Chemical. A vessel is 'hermetically sealed' by melting a portion of it in the blow-pipe flame and closing the orifice with its own material, which solidifies on cooling.

HYDROGEN (Gr. ὕδωρ, water; γεννάω, I produce). 'The water-producer;' the lightest of known bodies; one of the elements of water and of the acids generally.

HYGROMETER (Gr. ὑγρόs, wet, moist; μέτρον). An instrument for measuring the moisture of the air.

HYPOTHESIS (Gr. ὑπό, under; τίθημι, I place). 'Any supposition which we make (either without actual evidence, or on evidence avowedly insufficient) in order to endeavour to deduce from it conclusions in accordance with facts which are known to be real; under the idea that if the conclusions to which the hypothesis leads are known truths, the hypothesis itself either must be, or at least is likely to be, true. (J. S. Mill, 'Logic,' vol. ii. p. 8.)

IGNEOUS (Lat. *ignis*, fire). Applied to rocks whose materials have been consolidated from the molten state.

IMPETUS (Lat.). The force of a body in motion which must be overcome in order to bring the body to rest.

IMPINGE (Lat. *impingo*, I strike against).

IMPONDERABLE (Lat. *in*, not; *pondus*, weight). Without weight.

INCANDESCENT (Lat. *in + candesco*, to begin to glow). Glowing with a red or white heat.

INCIDENT (Lat. *in + cado*, I fall). Applied to a ray of heat or light as it falls upon a surface.

INCREMENT (Lat. *incrementum*, increase). Increase by a definite quantity.

INDEX (Lat.). A pointer or indicator.

INTERMITTENT (Lat. *inter*, between; *mitto*, I send). Acting at intervals.

KINETIC (Gr. κινέω, I set in motion). Applied to any form of energy which produces motion.

LATENT (Lat. *lateo*, I lie hid). Applied to heat which on passing into a body ceases to affect its temperature.

LIQUEFACTION (Lat. *liqueo*, to be fluid; *facio*, I make). Passage into the liquid state of a gas or vapour.

MECHANICAL (Gr. μηχανή, an artificial device, or contrivance). Applied to any device for doing work or directing energy; of the nature of a machine.

Glossary.

MERCURIAL (Lat. *mercurialis*, pertaining to Mercury). Composed of quicksilver.

MERCURY (Lat. *Mercurius*; Gr. 'Ερμῆς). Quicksilver, a white heavy metal, which is a liquid between temperatures of $-39°$ and $350°$ C.

METEORITES. (Gr. μετά, change; ἐώρα, anything suspended). Mineral masses attracted from interstellar space to the earth.

MOLECULE (Fr. dim. of Lat. *moles*, a mass). The smallest particle of a body that can exist as such in a free state.

NEBULAR (Lat. *nebula*, vapour). The *nebular hypothesis* supposes that the whole universe once existed in the condition of extremely attenuated vapour ('nebular fluid'), and that our sun and its planets, as well as all the worlds scattered through the starry depths, have been formed by the gradual condensation and cooling of this fluid.

NORMAL (Lat. *norma*, rule). According with the rule or law. In mathematics the line which is perpendicular to a plane surface, or to the tangential plane of a spherical surface.

OXIDE. A binary compound containing oxygen. *Oxidation*, the process of combination with oxygen.

OXYGEN (Gr. ὀξύς, sharp; γεννάω, I produce). Lit. the acid-producer; the most widely distributed body in nature; the supporter of combustion in the air; one of the elements of water and of oxides generally.

PARTICLES (Lat. *particula*, a small part). In physics, the smallest parts into which a body can be divided.

PERCUSSION (Lat. *percutio*, I strike). Striking together.

PHENOMENON, pl. PHENOMENA (Gr. φαίνομαι, I appear, come to light). In science anything that can be made a matter of observation.

PHYSICIST. One skilled in the investigation of physical laws.

PHYSICS (Gr. τὰ φυσικά, natural things; φύσις, nature). Synonymous with 'Natural Philosophy.' The investigation of the general properties of bodies.

PNEUMATIC (Gr. πνεῦμα, air, wind). Relating to air and gases generally.

POTENTIAL (Lat. *potens*, powerful). Applied to energy not in actual operation, but capable of being developed into 'kinetic' energy.

PRÆTER (Lat.) Beyond. 'Præter-scientific,' beyond the range of demonstrable knowledge.

PYROMETER (Gr. πῦρ, fire + μέτρον). An instrument for measuring very high temperatures.

RADIATE (Lat. *radio*). To emit rays or lines of light or heat from any point or surface. Substantive, 'radiation'; adjective, 'radiant.'

RECUPERATION (Lat. *recupero*, I recover). Recovery, compensation.

Glossary.

REFLECTION (Lat. *re+flecto*, I bend). Throwing back of rays of light or heat from the surface of a mirror.

REFRACTION (Lat. *re+frango*, I break). Change in the direction of a ray of light by the influence of the medium through which it passes.

RESPIRATION (Lat. *re+spiro*, I breathe). The act or process of breathing; aëration of the blood.

RETINA (Lat. *rete*, net). The expansion of the *optic nerve* at the back of the internal cavity of the eye, on which optical images are formed.

ROTATE (Lat. *roto*, from *rota*, a wheel). To turn round on an axis.

SATURATION (Lat. *saturo*, I fill). State of repletion; a space in connection with a liquid is said to be 'saturated' when evaporation has filled the space to the normal tension of the vapour of the liquid; air is 'saturated' with moisture when the slightest addition of vapour would cause precipitation; a magnet is 'saturated' when it is magnetised to the greatest possible degree.

SCIENCE (Lat. *scientia*, knowledge). Systematised knowledge of the phenomena and laws of nature, and of the means of extending that knowledge.

SENSATION (Lat. *sentio*, I feel). Sensations are the states of consciousness produced by the direct action of things upon the organs of sense.

SPECTRUM (Lat., an appearance). An optical appearance obtained by the dispersion of a ray of light into its component colours.

SPHEROIDAL (Gr. σφαῖρα, a globe; εἶδος, form). Approximating to the form of a sphere.

SUPERFICIAL (Lat. *super+facies*, face). Pertaining to a plane surface; having two dimensions, length and breadth.

TEMPERATURE (Lat. *temperatura*, due measure, proportion). Degree or proportion of sensible heat.

THERMOMETRY (Gr. θερμός + μέτρον). The measurement of the *temperature* of bodies.

VACUUM (Lat. *vacuus*, empty). An enclosed space entirely destitute of air or any other substance. '*Torricellian vacuum*,' the space above the mercurial column of the barometer, named from Torricelli (died 1647).

VELOCITY (Lat. *velox*, swift). The number of units of space which a body moving uniformly passes through in unit of time.

VITREOUS (Lat. *vitrum*, glass). Having the properties of glass.

VOLATILE (Lat. *volo*, I fly). Evaporating readily by the mere absorption of heat. Liquids which assume the aëriform state only as the result of chemical decomposition are called *fixed liquids*.

QUESTIONS.

The writing out of answers by the pupils, *in their own words*, to the following questions is strongly recommended, as well as the working of the examples where mathematical calculation is required, and, where practicable, the performance of all the experiments, even the simplest. Some of them have been written for this work; others reprinted from a variety of sources, more especially from the examination-papers of the 'Department of Science and Art,' and from papers set in Rugby School, which have been kindly supplied to the author by J. M. Wilson, Esq., M.A. They are intended to stimulate reference to larger works, as well as to test accuracy of knowledge of what is contained in this one.

CHAPTER I.

1. In the artillery-trials at Shoeburyness a sheet of flame is often seen at the moment when a shot strikes a target. Explain this.

2. Explain the use of a poker in a common fire; and the increase of heat in a smith's fire by the use of bellows.

3. What is a meteorite? What is considered to be the cause of its brilliancy?

4. What are the thermal effects of (1) hammering a piece of iron on an anvil; (2) stretching a piece of metallic wire?

5. Describe (with examples) the general characters which distinguish solids, liquids, and gases.

6. Write down the definition of heat according to modern theory.

7. Distinguish between *atoms* and *molecules*; between *heat* and the *sensation of heat*.

8. Explain precisely the term *temperature*. What is the use of a thermometer?

9. Give as many instances as you can of the conversion of mechanical force into heat.

10. What circumstances do you know of which determine the amount of heat generated by an electric current?

Questions. 109

11. Describe an experiment to illustrate the production of heat by electricity.

12. Describe the process of combustion in an ordinary gas-flame. What artificial contrivances are there for intensifying its heat?

13. How would you explain the fact that a wax-candle burns away as fast at the top of Mont Blanc as at its foot, but with a flame much less luminous?

14. How is it that in cold climates the human blood retains its proper temperature?

15. Describe as many instances as you can of the production of heat by chemical action.

16. Is *temperature* a quantity or a quality? Give your reasons.

CHAPTER II.

1. How are the two fixed points on the thermometric scale determined? What reasons necessitate the determination of the lower point first?

2. Describe fully the mode of filling and graduating a thermometer. What is meant by the calibration of the tube?

3. Describe some *maximum*, *minimum*, and *differential* thermometer.

4. What are the Centigrade and Fahrenheit thermometers? Why are they so named?

5. Make for yourself formulæ for the conversion of readings on either of the other scales into the corresponding readings on Réaumur's.

6. What are the readings on the other two scales which correspond respectively to 70° F. and 105° C.?

7. Why is water an unsuitable liquid for thermometric use? What are the limits of temperature to the use of mercury?

8. Describe the air-thermometer. What would be its natural zero, if air expands between the temperature of 0° C. and 100° C. in the ratio of $1 : 1\cdot3665$?

9. Required the readings in C. and F. degrees for 10° and $-30°$ Réaumur.

10. Mercury freezes at a temperature which has the same reading on both C. and F. scale: find it.

11. What is meant by *absolute zero*? What is the absolute temperature which corresponds to the 0° F. and 0° C.?

12. Describe Breguet's metallic thermometer.

13. What are the advantages and disadvantages of the air-thermometer?

14. How many degrees of Celsius are equal to 54° F.? How many degrees of Fahr. equal to −20° C.? How many of Réaumur to 100° F. and to 100° C.?

15. Describe some common form of pyrometer and explain its use.

16. Explain the use of 'Gravesande's Ring.'

17. Describe as many simple cases as you can of the 'expansion of heat.'

18. How would you explain (by reference to Art. 38) the fracture of glass under change of temperature when a silver or brass wire is soldered into it, but not when a platinum or iron wire is so inserted?

19. Describe the construction of the deep-sea thermometer. Why is the peculiarity in its construction necessary?

20. A stopper may often be loosened by warming the neck of a bottle: why is this?

21. Two *straight* plates, one of steel the other of brass, are riveted together at both ends. What would be the effect of heating the combination?

22. A litre of water at its maximum density is found, on being heated to 100° C., to fill 1·04315 litres: find its mean coefficient of expansion. How far does this represent the facts of the case?

23. Why does ice float? What influence has the depth of still water upon congelation?

24. The mean sp. gr. of sea-water being 1·0275 (Herschel), show that the density of ice is about ·9 that of sea-water. What portion of an iceberg projects above the surface?

25. The length of the railway from London to Edinburgh being 400 miles, and the variations of temperature in winter and summer 50° C., calculate the variation that would occur in the length of the metal, if continuous. How is this avoided in practice?

26. Prove the rule:

'Cubical expansion of a solid = 3 × linear expansion.'

27. Describe the Gridiron pendulum and the Mercurial pendulum.

28. Estimate the proportionate lengths required in a gridiron pendulum; (1) when wrought iron and silver are used; (2) when zinc and bronze are used.

29. Demonstrate the formulæ for correction of volume of a gas for (1) normal pressure; (2) normal temperature.

30. If some gas occupies 100 ccm. at 17° C., what will be its volume at 0° C.? And what if its pressure had been changed from 730 mm. to 760 mm.?

Questions.

31. One litre of a gas is measured off at 20° C. and a pressure of 765 mm.: required its volume at the normal pressure and temperature.

32. State clearly the laws of Boyle and Charles.

33. A gas occupies 100 ccm. at 0° C. and 760 mm. pressure: what volume will it occupy at 10° C. and a pressure of 740 mm.?

34. The coefficient of expansion of gaseous bodies being known for 1° C., find it for 1° F. and 1° R.

35. A gas fills 5 litres at the normal pressure and 60° F.: what is its volume at the temperature of freezing water?

36. 50 ccm. of a gas are cooled down (at constant pressure) from 10° C. to −10° C.: what is the resulting volume?

37. 50 ccm. of a gas at 700 mm. pressure are subjected to an additional pressure of 100 mm., the temperature remaining unaltered: required the alteration in the volume of the gas.

38. A litre of gas is cooled down from 64° F. to 0° F. at constant pressure: required the resulting volume.

39. Find the length of a bar of brass at 40° C. which at 62° C. is 29 inches long. What alteration would occur in the length of the bar, the temperature being lowered through the same number of F. degrees?

40. How is heat most easily propagated through liquids and gases?

41. A litre of air at 0° C. weighs 1·2932 grammes: what will a litre of it weigh when heated to 20° C.?

42. Given the height of the barometric column 29·9 inches, the sp. gr. of mercury 13·56, and the weight of a cubic foot of water at 4° C. = 1,000 ozs. Find the pressure of the atmosphere per sq. foot.

43. A volume of a gas at 37° C. is 125 ccm.: what will be its volume at 27° C., the pressure remaining unchanged?

44. Describe some method of accurately determining the linear expansion of a solid.

45. Prove the rule:
'Areal expansion of a solid = 2 × linear expansion.'

46. If a clock has a brass pendulum, find how much it will gain or lose per day by a change of temperature from 10° to 25° C. (Time of oscillation of pendulum varies as square root of its length.)

47. A cubic inch of brass at 62° F. weighs 2,019 grains, what would a cubic inch weigh at 32° C.?

48. Distinguish between *real* and *apparent* expansion of liquids, and describe a method for ascertaining the absolute expansion of mercury.

49. What is the abnormal case of the expansion of water? Trace some of its consequences in the economy of nature.

50. Describe Major Williams' experiment on freezing water's expansive force.

51. If 273 litres of a gas are at 0°C., to what temperature must it be heated to fill 300 litres?

52. A gas measures 536 litres at −5° C., to what temperature must it be raised to fill 600 litres?

53. 1 grm. of hydrogen occupies 11·2 litres at normal pressure and temperature: required its volume (1) at 15° C.; (2) at −15° C.

CHAPTER III.

1. A vessel contains ice and ice-cold water, another contains lead partly molten and partly solid, and pressure is applied to both: what is the difference of the result in the two cases?

2. Explain the theory of freezing-mixtures with examples.

3. State the laws of fusion.

4. Explain the expression—'latent heat of fusion.'

5. Describe the method of obtaining the latent heat of fusion of a substance. Illustrate your answer by the case of water.

6. A pound of ice at 0° C. is placed in a pound of water at 96° C.: what will be the temperature of the water when fusion is complete? What if 3 pounds of water were used?

7. 2 pounds of ice are dissolved in 7 pounds of water at 60° C.: required the temperature of the liquid after fusion.

8. How much water at 100° C. must be added to 130 grms. of ice at 0° C. to convert it into water at 5° C.?

9. Show how sp. gr. enables us to determine whether during the fusion of a given solid it expands or contracts.

10. Define a 'thermal unit.'

11. What is meant by the 'vitreous state'? Give examples.

12. What is an 'alloy'? What its effect upon fusion?

13. How many thermal units are required to melt 1 cwt. of ice at 0° C. How many pounds of water would the same quantity of heat raise from 0° C. to 100° C.?

14. Refer to the table of fusion-temperatures (Art. 50), and construct a corresponding table expressing the temperatures (1) in F. degrees; (2) in R. degrees.

15. Can you show why water in summer, if kept in a *porous* earthenware vessel, is cooler than if kept in a glazed vessel?

16. State, and give a theoretical proof of, the laws of evaporation.

Questions.

17. What is meant by the 'tension' of a vapour?

18. How did Faraday liquefy certain gases? What is the meaning of the term 'permanent' as applied to a gas?

19. Give some account of Andrews's researches on the relation between the liquid and gaseous conditions of carbon dioxide.

20. What is (1) the 'critical temperature;' (2) the 'critical point'?

21. State clearly what is meant by the 'latent heat of evaporation.'

22. Describe a method for ascertaining the latent heat of steam.

23. How much steam is required to raise a hundred pounds of water from 52° to 90° C.?

24. Into the Torricellian vacuum of two tubes, water and ether are passed up: state the effect in each case.

25. Describe instances of the use of evaporation to produce cold. How do you account for this?

26. Describe the construction and action of the cryophorus, and of some freezing machine which acts on the same principle.

27. What means are there for determining the amount of vapour in the air? What is the dew-point? and the depression of the dew-point?

28. Explain fully the phenomenon of boiling. How would you account for the explosive boiling of geysers?

29. Explain the use of the wet-bulb thermometer.

30. What will be the temperature of 30 pounds of water taken at 10° C., after injecting one pound of steam at 100° C.?

31. Calculate the volumetric ratio of a given quantity of water to the steam at 100° C., generated by its ebullition.

32. Explain and illustrate the meaning of the term *hygrometry*. What is the 'hygrometric state'?

33. Carbon dioxide is pumped at high pressure into a strong reservoir at temperature 31° C.: what form will the gas take in the reservoir?

34. State the various conditions that affect the boiling-point of a liquid.

35. Describe an experiment to prove the third law of ebullition.

36. A thermometer is placed in ice at a temperature of −20° C. The ice is first heated till it all melts; the water is then heated till it is all converted into steam. Describe the changes indicated by the thermometer throughout the entire process.

37. It was observed by De Saussure that at an altitude of 15,650 ft. on Mont Blanc, water boiled at a temperature of 185·8° F. Explain this; and calculate the average difference of level required to effect an alteration in the boiling-point of 1° F. and of 1° C.

38. I place water, alcohol, and ether in succession upon my hand, and experience cold in different degrees: explain this.

39. An ounce of steam at 212° F. is injected into one pound of water at 53° F.; what will be the temperature of the mixture?

40. Explain the difference between boiling and simmering.

41. One ounce of steam at 100° C. is passed into 9 ounces of water at 10° C. and condensed. What will be the temperature of the 10 ounces of water?

42. What is a 'volatile' liquid? What a 'fixed' liquid?

43. Carbonic anhydride gas may be procured in the liquid and solid form. Explain how.

44. State the correct use of the terms 'gas,' 'vapour;' illustrate your answer by the case of water.

45. In what different ways may the evaporation of a liquid be accelerated without applying heat?

46. State distinctly the laws of ebullition.

47. Water is placed over oil of vitriol in the receiver of an air-pump; the air is then gradually withdrawn. What effect will this have upon the temperature of (1) the water; (2) the oil of vitriol?

48. What do you understand by (1) the saturation of a *space*; (2) the saturation of a *liquid*?

49. What different arrangements can you describe for freezing water in a warm room?

50. Describe a simple experiment which shows that the boiling-point is affected by pressure.

51. Explain fully the action of a 'digester,' and of a 'high-pressure engine.'

CHAPTER IV.

1. State clearly what is meant by the 'flow of heat' across a wall.

2. Define 'conduction of heat.' Explain the thermal condition of a body that has attained the *permanent* state of temperature.

3. What is meant by the term 'co-efficient of conductivity'?

4. Give instances of good and bad conductors, and of phenomena explained by the different conductivities of bodies.

5. How is the low conductivity of gases proved? Describe an experiment which shows hydrogen to be a marked exception.

6. State exactly the difference between 'conduction' and 'convection.'

7. Describe some experiments to show the difference between good and bad conductors of heat.

8. The 'Cornish' boiler is so constructed that the furnace is contained within a large tube which is surrounded by the water of the boiler. Show that this is an economical arrangement.

9. I take a cylinder composed partly of brass, partly of wood. I wrap a piece of white paper tightly round the junction of the two materials and hold it for a short time in a flame. The paper covering one substance is charred more quickly than that which covers the other. Which part will be charred most? and why?

10. What do you understand by the 'spheroidal condition' of water? How may it be explained?

11. Explain the action of the safety-lamp.

12. You are provided with bars of copper, gold, silver, and platinum, and are required to devise a means for ascertaining their thermal conductivities: how would you proceed?

13. You place one hand in mercury, the other hand in water, both liquids being at the same temperature: the hand in the mercury feels colder than the hand in the water. Why?

14. What is the scientific meaning of the term 'warm-clothing'?

15. Explain the use of a 'jacket' of felt and wood around the cylinder of a steam-engine.

16. What is the reason why in a Turkish bath, at a temperature of 200° F., the human body remains at a temperature of 100° F.?

17. Mention as many instances as you can of the practical application of the principle of conduction.

18. How would you prove water to be a bad conductor?

19. Write from memory the conductivities of gold, silver, iron, copper, and lead.

CHAPTER V.

1. Distinguish carefully between *temperature* and *quantity* of heat. Illustrate your answer by the case of water and mercury.

2. Give accurate definitions of the terms *specific heat* and *capacity for heat*.

3. Write down from memory the specific heats of water, alcohol, mercury, iron, and lead.

4. 15 grammes of silver at 90° C. are agitated with ten grammes of water at 10° C., and the resulting temperature is 16·3° C.; find the sp. heat of silver.

Solution.—The silver has been cooled $(90 - 16\cdot 3)° = 73\cdot 7°$, and in parting with this temperature has raised the water $6\cdot 3°$.

∴ if the weights of water and silver were the same we should get—

$$\text{sp. heat of silver} = \frac{6\cdot 3}{73\cdot 7}.$$

But the ratio of the wt. of the water to the wt. of the silver is 2 : 3.

$$\therefore \text{sp. heat of silver} = \frac{6\cdot 3}{73\cdot 7} \times \frac{2}{3} = \cdot 056.$$

5. An ounce of bismuth is transferred from boiling water to 3 ounces of water at 50° F., raising its temperature to 51·5° F. Determine the sp. heat of bismuth.

6. 10 grammes of a gas at 100° C. pass through a tube in a vessel of water and issue from the water at 20° C., raising thereby 100 grammes of water from 15° to 17° C. Find the sp. heat of the gas.

7. A pound of lead at 212° F. is placed in 1 pound of water at 57° F., the resulting temperature is 62° F. Find the sp. heat of the lead.

8. One gramme of iron at 100° is thrown into 1 gramme of water at 0°, and the temperature of the whole is finally 10·22°. Determine the sp. heat of iron.

9. A pound of iron at 100° C. is immersed in 2 pounds of water at 16° C., and the resulting temperature of the whole is 20·5° C. Calculate from these data the sp. heat of iron.

10. A pound of iron at 100° is immersed in a pound of water at 50°; how many degrees will the temperature of the water be raised?

11. A pound of cold iron is placed in a pound of water at 212° F. The water loses 5° of temperature. How many has the iron gained?

12. A pound of lead at 50° C. is immersed in a pound of water at 0° C.: what will be the resulting temperature of both?

13. What are the sources of 'errors of experiment' in the calorimetric method of mixture?

14. A cwt. of ice at 0° C. has to be melted: what weight of steam at 100° C. must be employed?

15. A pond is calculated to contain 1000 tons of ice at 0° C.: what weight of water at 50° C. will melt it?

16. What weight of steam at 100° C. is needed for the fusion of 1 ton of ice?

17. What weight of mercury at 100° C. will melt a pound of ice at 0° C.?

18. State Dulong and Petit's law of atomic heats. Given the atomic wts.—Hydrogen = 1; Nitrogen = 14; Oxygen = 12; Chlorine = 35·5;

and the sp. heat of hydrogen = 3·409 ; find the sp. heats of the three other gases.

19. Ten grammes of oxygen have to be cooled from 100° C. to 0° C. What weight of ice is required for the purpose?

20. What quantity of heat will be required to raise the temperature of 100 grammes of oxygen from 0° C. to 100° C. at constant pressure?

21. What quantity of heat (how many thermal units) is required to raise 90 grammes of hydrogen from 0° C. to 300° C.?

22. Show the importance of the high sp. heat of water.

23. Repeat the experiment represented in fig. 26, substituting a sheet of ice for the cake of wax, and using balls of silver, brass, and glass.

24. What do we mean by
'The heat of combustion of hydrogen = 34,500 thermal units'?

25. A cwt. of ice has to be melted: how much hydrogen would by its combustion give out enough heat for the purpose?

26. How much hydrogen must you burn to heat 100 grammes of water from 0° C. to 100° C.? How much more to heat the steam up to 120° C.?

27. I have to heat 50 grammes of water from 10° C. to 90° C. What weight of hydrogen must be burnt for this purpose?

28. I heat a ball of lead and one of iron to the same temperature, and place them both on snow: state the proportionate depths to which they will sink.

29. Short cylinders (of equal length) of iron and bismuth are coated at one end with wax. Their opposite ends are then equally heated, and the wax on the bismuth is found to be melted before the wax on the iron. How do you reconcile this fact with the statement in Art. 84, that the conductivity of iron is to the conductivity of bismuth as 11·9 : 1·9?

CHAPTER VI.

1. Contrast the transmission of heat by *conduction* and *radiation*.
2. Give an *à priori* proof of the 'law of inverse squares.'
3. Explain the *theory of exchanges* with examples.
4. What are the relations of the *absorptive, reflective,* and *radiating* powers of any given substance?
5. Describe some experiments or natural phenomena which illustrate the distinction between *dark* and *luminous* heat.
6. Mention substances which are opaque to heat and transparent to light; and the converse

7. Explain by what arrangement the sun's heat could be brought to a focus by a lens of ice without melting the ice. What would result from coating it with iodine?

8. State some of the thermal uses of aqueous vapour in the air.

9. Why is glass used for hothouses and fire-screens?

10. Why as a rule are light clothes cooler in summer than dark ones?

11. Describe an arrangement for dispersing a ray of white solar light into its component colours.

12. State what you know regarding the different kinds of 'rays' emitted by the sun.

13. Describe the relative heating-powers of the different parts of the solar spectrum.

14. Ice is formed on clear nights in India when the temperature is $15°$ or $16°$ F. above the freezing-point. How is this possible? What difference would a cloudy sky make?

15. What do you understand by radiant heat as distinguished from light? How do they resemble each other?

16. Franklin once exposed bits of cloth of different colours on the snow to the sun's rays, and found that the darker the cloth the deeper it sank in the snow. Give the explanation of this.

17. Is it a fact that dark bodies are always more highly heated by the sun than light ones? If not, explain why.

18. Explain the accumulation of heat in glass-houses, and apply your knowledge to explain the influence of the earth's atmosphere upon the temperature of the earth.

19. State fully the atmospheric conditions favourable to the copious deposition of dew. What effect have clouds and winds upon this phenomenon?

20. A thermometer placed in an open box, and exposed to the sun, rises $80°$ F. A glass cover is placed on the box, and the temperature rises to $120°$ F. Explain this.

21. What property of rock-salt makes it extremely valuable for researches in radiant heat?

22. Describe the effects of plates of glass, alum, and ice, in absorbing and transmitting heat of different qualities.

23. What difference is there in the effects of radiant heat, according to the nature of its source?

24. What is the meaning of the term 'diathermanous'?

25. Explain by the aid of a diagram the meaning of 'conjugate foci.'

26. State the 'Laws of Reflection.'

27. Show experimentally that radiant heat is independent of light

CHAPTER VII.

1. A block of stone weighing half a ton falls from the top of a tower 50 feet high: required the number of thermal units generated by its arrest.

Solution:—It follows from Art. 113 that

1 pound falling 772 feet acquires a moving force = 1 thermal unit.
∴ 1,120 ,,   ,, 772 ,,   ,,   ,,   = 1,120   ,,
and 1,120 ,,   ,, 50 ,,   ,,   ,,   = $1,120 \times \frac{50}{772}$,,
∴ No. of thermal units produced = 72·5.

2. Supposing the sp. heat of the stone in Ex. 1 to be ·25; what elevation of temperature will the stone undergo?

Solution:—Every pound of water in falling 772 feet generates heat sufficient to raise its temperature 1° F.

∴ for a fall of water through 50 feet we have

772 : 50 :: 1 : x (= ·065° F. elevation of temp. of water).

But since the sp. heat of the stone is ·25 we have

·25 : 1 :: ·065° : z (= ·26° F.) ;

where ·26° F. = elevation of the temperature of the stone, supposing (which would not be true in practice) that all the heat was imparted to the block.

(In 3, 4, 5, 6, *it is assumed that one-half the heat generated enters the body which is arrested.*)

3. A piece of zinc falls from the height of 500. Through what temperature Fahr. will it be raised by the arrest of its motion?

4. If a mass of iron fall through 1,000 feet, through how many degrees Cent. will its temperature be raised by arrest of its motion?

5. Mercury is poured from one vessel into another 10 feet below: how many degrees Fahr. is its temperature raised?

6. Calculate in a similar manner the elevation of temperature of each of the metals mentioned in the list on page 75, by a fall from a height of 100 ft.

7. A 68-pound cannon-ball strikes a target with a velocity of 1,400 feet per second. If all the heat generated by the collision were imparted to 68 lbs. of water at 60° F., what would be the rise of temperature of the water?

Solution:—If we substitute for the cannon-ball a body falling from rest until it acquires a velocity of 1,400 ft. per second, it is clear that the *mean* velocity of this body is, during its fall, 700 ft. per second.

If s = the space (in feet) fallen through, and t the number of seconds of the fall, we get $s = 700\,t$.

But by a simple dynamical formula

$$s = \tfrac{1}{2} g t^2$$

(where $g = 32\cdot2$ = the increment of velocity per second of a falling body)

$$\therefore\ 16\cdot1 \times t^2 = 700\,t.$$

$$\text{whence } t = \frac{700}{16\cdot1} = 43\cdot5 \text{ seconds.}$$

But $s = 700\,t, = 700 \times 43\cdot5 = 30{,}450$ feet,

∴ the force of the ball in motion at the moment of collision
= the force required to lift 68 pounds through 30,450 feet,
= 30,450 × 68 foot-pounds.

∴ rise of temperature of 1 pound of water $= \dfrac{30{,}450 \times 68}{772}$ deg. Fahr.

and ,,   ,,   68 ,,   ,, $= \dfrac{30{,}450 \times 68}{772 \times 68} = 39\cdot4°$ Fahr.

Hence the resulting temperature = 60° + 39·4° = 99·4° Fahr.

8. A weight of a ton is lifted by a steam-engine through a height of 386 feet: what is the amount of heat consumed in the act?

9. A block of rock weighing 1,500 pounds is loosened by frost from the top of a precipice 500 feet high, and falls into the valley below. How much heat is generated by the fall?

10. A block of stone weighing 1 ton falls from a height of 300 feet upon a glacier. Estimate the amount of ice melted by the fall, assuming that half the heat generated enters the ice.

11. Define the term 'foot-pound,' 'mechanical equivalent.'

12. Describe some of the experiments by which Joule ascertained the mechanical equivalent of heat.

13. What do you understand by *conservation of energy*?

14. Give as many instances as you can of the conversion of *kinetic* into *potential* energy.

16. Give as many instances as you can of the conversion of heat into work.

17. What can, and what cannot, a machine do?

18. From what height must a body of water fall, in order that its temperature may be raised 1° F., or 1° C.? From this ascertain the heights through which each of the solids mentioned on page 75 must fall to produce the same alteration of temperature.

MISCELLANEOUS QUESTIONS.

1. Enumerate the advantages and disadvantages of the employment of mercury for thermometric purposes.

2. When we wish to compare the thermal effects of solar radiation at two different times or places, we use a thermometer coated with *lamp-black*: when we wish to ascertain the true temperature of the air at any place, we use a thermometer with the bulb coated with *polished silver*. Give the reasons.

3. Why is the average cold of January and February greater than that of December in the northern hemisphere?

4. What are the methods of finding the specific heat of a solid? What errors are to be guarded against?

5. What is the exact meaning of the following statements:

'The specific heat of hydrogen is 3·2936.
'The latent heat of water is 79·25.'?

6. I blow air from bellows upon the face of the thermo-pile; I then direct upon it a jet from air compressed in a box. What will be the result as shown by the galvanometer in each case? and why?

7. Classify the consequences of applying heat to a body. Which of these are used as measures of temperature and of quantity of heat?

8. What is *regelation*? Explain by it the formation of ice on a frequented foot-path after a fall of snow. How does this apply to the formation of glacier-ice?

9. In the city of Nice it is remarked that you may be cold in the shade, while the moment you step into the sunshine the heat is found to be great: explain this.

10. Can you conceive it possible by means of an atmosphere to raise the temperature of a planet more distant than the earth from the sun to the earth's temperature? If so, explain how.

11. State the considerations on which the absolute zero is founded. What is the lowest observed temperature? How is it obtained?

12. State and illustrate what is meant by Athermancy and Diathermancy.

13. A black hat is heated by the solar rays *more* than a white one: what is the reason? Dark iodine is, however, heated by the same rays *less* than white sugar: what is the reason?

14. State what you know regarding the radiation of heat from the earth, and the effects of this radiation.

15. Give a clear statement of what you understand by the *radiation*, *reflection*, and *absorption* of heat.

16. State clearly how you suppose winds are produced.

17. State clearly how you suppose rain to be formed from the beginning of its formation to the end.

18. State clearly how you suppose hoar-frost to be formed.

19. How do you account for hail and snow?

20. You are furnished with an ounce of each of the following metals, and are required to determine their specific heats: gold, silver, copper, iron, lead, bismuth. How would you proceed?

21. You are required to determine experimentally the distribution of heat in the solar spectrum, and to exhibit the distribution graphically by a properly plotted curve. How would you proceed?

22. Upon what observed data are we led to believe in the great heat of the earth's interior? Show how we should be led to the same conclusion on *à priori* grounds.

23. How is the heat of a fire produced? How is the heat of your own body produced?

24. State fully all the reasons for the precautions adopted in graduating a thermometer.

25. What is the effect on the height of the column of mercury of inclining the tube (1) of a barometer; (2) of a thermometer? (Given the hydrostatic law: 'The pressure of a liquid column varies as its vertical height.')

26. Describe the thermo-pile.

27. Express in Cent. degrees the following readings on the Fahr. scale: $-10°$, $2°$, $180°$, $212°$.

28. A gas occupies 150 ccm. at 730 mm. pressure: what will be its volume at 780 mm. pressure, temperature constant?

29. Give examples of the effects of expansion and contraction of metals.

30. The edge of a cubical block of a solid expands when heated in the ratio of $1 : 1\cdot01$; find its cubical expansion accurately and approximately.

31. Explain and illustrate the expression: 'Heat and work are mutually convertible.'

32. Why in mountain-regions is precipitation of moisture greater than in the plains?

33. In the construction of chimneys what are the main points to be considered?

34. A gas measures 100 ccm. at normal pressure; what will be its volume at 700 mm. and at 800 mm.?

35. A gas measures 1,000 ccm. at $-10°$ C.; what will it measure at $100°$ C.?

Questions.

36. A block of pure ice weighs 500 grammes: find its volume in ccm.

37. It is often observed that at the end of a shower the window-panes of an inhabited room are bedewed on the interior. How may this be accounted for?

38. Explain why ether spray produces great cold.

39. Describe the changes of volume that water undergoes in its passage from ice at $-20°$ C. to steam under a pressure of one atmosphere.

40. What atmospheric conditions mainly determine the accumulation, dispersion, and precipitation of clouds. Distinguish between 'cloud' and 'vapour.'

41. Give instances of condensable and non-condensable gases.

42. Find the corresponding temperatures on the Fahr. scale for the boiling-points given in Art. 72.

43. A salt is decomposed by heat: what becomes of the heat?

44. Two vessels of water are heated, the one at the top, the other at the bottom. In what different ways is heat transmitted through the water?

45. An incrustation of carbonate of lime is often formed on the interior of engine-boilers from spring-water. How does this affect the necessary consumption of fuel?

46. Given Cent. readings,

$$-140°, -40°, -5°, 5°, 45°, 120°.$$

convert them into Fahr. readings.

47. Find the total increase in length of the rails from London to Liverpool (200 miles) corresponding to a change of temperature from $32°$ to $82°$ F.

48. Distinguish between *real* and *apparent* expansion of liquids.

49. 15 litres are collected at $25°$ C. What volume will the same gas occupy at $-5°$ C.?

50. A quantity of gas has to be collected at $16°$ C. and 750 mm. pressure, which shall occupy 100 ccm. at $0°$ C. and 760 mm. pressure. How much must be collected?

51. It being a fact well known to physiologists that the energy of the body rises and falls in proportion to the supply of oxygen to the blood; show that neglect of ventilation entails loss upon the owner of a factory or workshop, as well as upon the workpeople. What general principles are to be borne in mind in ventilating a building?

52. Why can a snowball be made from fresh-fallen snow better than from snow which has been exposed to a very severe frost?

53. Show that rain is an agent for equalizing the earth's temperature.

54. 'The critical temperature of carbon dioxide is 30·9° C.' Explain this.

55. What becomes of the heat taken from the water which is frozen in the cryophorus?

56. State distinctly the laws of ebullition and evaporation.

57. Why is wicker-work or matting placed under hot dishes on a dinner-table?

58. Given Fahr. readings:

$$-460°, -300°, -40°, 39°, 140°, 172°, 200°, 360°.$$

convert them into Cent. readings.

59. In warming a house by hot water, why can you not place the boiler at the top of the house?

60. How does frost produce leakage in water-pipes?

61. Describe the methods of ascertaining the tension (elasticity) of aqueous vapour (1) for temperatures below 100° C.; (2) for temperatures above 100° C.

62. Distinguish between the liquid state of ammonia and a solution of ammonia.

63. I take a beaker full of a supersaturated solution of sulphate of lime and drop into it a minute portion of the salt. Crystallization at once commences, and a thermo-pile applied to the side of the beaker indicates heat. What does this prove?

64. You have given to you an ordinary mercury thermometer, a water thermometer, and a bath; and you are required to find the temperature of maximum density of water. How would you proceed?

ANSWERS TO EXAMPLES.

CHAPTER II.

(6) $21\frac{1}{8}$°C, $16·8$°R; 221°F; 84°R.
(8) -273°C.
(9) $12·5$°C, $54·5$°F; $-37·5$°C, $-35·5$°F.
(14) $12·2$°C, -4°F, $30·2$°R, 80°R.
(22) $·010435$ (cf. art. 46).
(25) $·224$ of a mile (cast iron).
   $·244$,, (wrought iron).
(31) $937·64$ ccm. (33) $106·46$ ccm.
(35) $4·45$ lit. (36) $46·47$ ccm.
(38) $884·48$ ccm. (39) $28·99$ ins.
(41) $1·205$ grs. (43) $120·97$ ccm.
(46) $13·536$ sec. (47) $2013·56$ grs.

CHAPTER III.

(6) $8·5$°C, $52·5$°C.
(7) $29\frac{1}{9}$°C. (8) $114·94$ gms.
(13) 8848 pound-units; $88·48$ lbs.
(23) $70·9$ pounds. (30) $22·2$°C.
(37) $597·33$ feet; $1075·19$ feet.
(39) $118·82$°F. (41) $72·6$°C.

CHAPTER V.

(5) $·028$. (6) $·25$.
(7) $·0\dot{3}$. (8, 9) $·11\dot{4}$.
(10) $5·12$. (11) $43·85$°.
(12) $1·5$°C. (14) $14·85$ pounds.
(15) 1580 tons.
(16) $278·24$ lbs. nearly.
(17) $23·7$ pounds. (19) $2·759$ gms.
(20) 2180 gramme-units.

CHAPTER V. (*continued*).

(21) 92043 gramme-units.
(25) $·255$ pounds of hydrogen.
(26) $·288$ grammes   ,,
    $·028$,,   ,,
(27) $·116$ grm.

CHAPTER VII.

(3) $3·37$°F. (4) $3·15$°C.
(5) $·19$°F.
(6) $1·27$°F, $1·15$°F, $0·80$°F,
    $2·11$°F, $1·14$°F, $0·70$°F,
    $1·15$°F, $0·55$°F, $0·69$°F,
    $0·58$°F, $2·02$°F, $2·02$°F,
    $2·08$°F, $0·68$°F.
(8) $622\frac{2}{3}$ units.
(9) 540 pound-units.
(10) $3·06$ pounds.

MISCELLANEOUS.

(27) $-23·3$°C, $-16·6$°C, $82·2$°C, 220°C.
(28) $140·39$ ccm.
(34) $108·57$ ccm.; 95 ccm.
(35) $1418·25$ ccm.
(46) -220°F, -40°F, 23°F, 41°F, 113°F, 248°F.
(47) $·0627$ mile. (49) $13·49$ litres.
(50) $106·78$ ccm.
(58) $-273\frac{1}{3}$°C, $-184\frac{4}{9}$°C, -40°C, $3·8$°C, 60°C, $77\frac{7}{9}$°C, $93\frac{1}{3}$°C, $182\frac{2}{9}$°C.

INDEX.

⁎ The Numbers refer to the *Articles.*

ABS

ABSOLUTE zero, absolute temperature, 27
Absorption of heat, 108
Air-thermometer, 24
Atom defined, 2

BAROMETRIC column, 32
Boiling point, how determined, 19; precautions necessary, 19, 73, 78; dependent upon atmospheric pressure, 72–75, pp. 97, 98
Boyle's Law, 26

CALIBRATION, 20
Calorimetry by mixture, fusion, and cooling, 96
Capacity for heat, 93 *et seq.*; definition of, 98
Carbonic anhydride (carbon dioxide), sometimes called carbonic acid, liquefied and solidified, 68
Carré's freezing machine, 63
Charles' Law, 27
Chemical action, a source of heat, 13; dissociation, the result of heat, 80
Chimneys, draught of, 29
Cloud and vapour, 58
Co-efficient of expansion, of gases, 27; of solids, 34–38; absolute and apparent in liquids, 42, 43
Combustion, 13-15
Compensating pendulums, 40
Condenser, 64

EVA

Conduction of heat, 83 *et seq.*; variable and permanent stages, 84; how measured, 84; illustrations, 85; practical applications, 86, 88
Conjugate foci, 111
Conservation of energy, 114
Convection of heat in liquids, 45
Critical point, 61
Cryophorus, 64

DARK and luminous heat, 102
Dew, 109
Dew-point, 65
Diathermanous bodies, 109
Digester, 74
Dissipation of energy, 115
Distillation, 79
Divisibility of matter, 2
Dulong and Petit's method for obtaining absolute expansion, 42; law of atomic heats, 97

EBULLITION, 72 *et seq.*; laws of, 77; circumstances that affect it, 78
Elasticity of vapours and gases, 4, 17, 26-28, 59-61
Electrical resistance a source of heat, 12
Energy; its universal distribution, 3; varieties, 3
Ether spray; its cooling effect, 67
Evaporation, 56 *et seq.*; laws of, 60

Index.

EXP

Expansion—of solids, 17, 34-40; of liquids, 17, 42-44; of gases, 17, 26-31

FACTOR of expansion, 27
Fire-balloon, 28
Flowers of sulphur, 71
Fluids characterised, 4
Foot-warmers, 98
Freezing-mixtures, 53, 68
Freezing-point; how found, 19; displacement of, 20
Friction a source of heat, 6
Fusion-laws, 51

GALVANOMETER, 25
Gases characterised, 4; diffusion of, 4; distinguished from 'vapours,' 61
Gaseous laws, 26, 27
Geysers, 30
Glass, its co-efficient of cubical expansion, 44
Gulf-stream, 45; its thermal effects, 70

HAIL, 71
Heat and Work, 48, 50, 74, 76, 80, 112, 113, 114
Heron's Fountain, 28
Hoar-frost, 109
Hydrogen, a good conductor, 91
Hygrometers, 65, 66

JOULE'S experiments, 113

KINETIC energy, 114

LAND and sea breezes, 30
Latent heat—of fusion, 50; of water, 52; of solution, 53; of evaporation, 70; of steam, 76
Lavoisier and Laplace's method of determining linear expansion, 35
Leslie's cube, its use in researches in latent heat, 106
Liquefaction of gases, 62

RAI

Liquefaction of solids, 50; how influenced by pressure, &c., 50
Liquids characterised, 4

MAJOR Williams' experiment on the expansive force of freezing water, 47
Maximum density of water, 46
Mechanical equivalent of heat, 113
Mercury—its use for thermometry, 18, 93; its absolute expansion, 42; apparent expansion, 43; freezing-point, 50; boiling-point, 72; its oxide reduced by heat, 80; its sp. heat, 93; effect of a film on radiation, 106
Meteoric phenomena resulting from expansion, 30, 31
Molecular motion, 3; energy, 3, 26
Molecule defined, 2
Mountain ranges, precipitation of moisture, 31

NATURE of heat, 1-5
Nebular hypothesis, 115
Normal pressure and temperature 32; correction for, 33

OXIDATION, a source of heat, 13

PERCUSSION, a source of heat, 7
Permanent gases, 49, 62
Physics, distinguished from chemistry, 2
Position of advantage, 114
Potential energy, 114
Pressure, a source of heat, 8
Pyrometer (Ferguson's), 34

RADIANT energy, 100 *et seq.*, how different from light, 101, 103
Radiation, law of inverse squares, 105
Rain, 71

Ratio of weight and volume of water to volume of steam generated, 81
Reflection, laws of, 110
Regelation, 50
Rock-salt, its diathermancy, 109
Rupert's drops, 39

SAFETY-LAMP, 88
Scales of graduation, 19
Simmering, 72
Snow, 71
Solar heat, 10
Solids characterised, 4
Specific heat, 93 *et seq.*; definition of, 99
Specific unit, 93
Spectrum, heat rays of, 102, 103
Spheroidal state, 90
Superheated steam, 61

TEMPERATURE defined, 5
Terrestrial heat, 11, 92

Theory of exchanges, 105
Thermal unit, 52
Thermometer defined, 5; its construction, 18; graduation of, 19; different scales, 19; differential, 21; maximum and minimum, 22; metallic, 23; air, 24; sources of error, 20; for deep-sea use, 20
Thermo-pile, 25
Torricellian vacuum, 60, 73, 100
Trade-winds, 30

VAPOUR density, 32
Ventilation, 29
Vitreous state, 54
Volatile bodies, 58

WATER, frozen in the air-pump, 64; its low conductivity proved, 89; how frozen in Bengal, 109
Wind, its drying effect, 57; cooling effect of a warm wind, 67

www.ingramcontent.com/pod-product-compliance
Lightning Source LLC
Chambersburg PA
CBHW022134160426
43197CB00009B/1280